AF470909

A Little Art Education

by Lynn Barber

CHEERIO

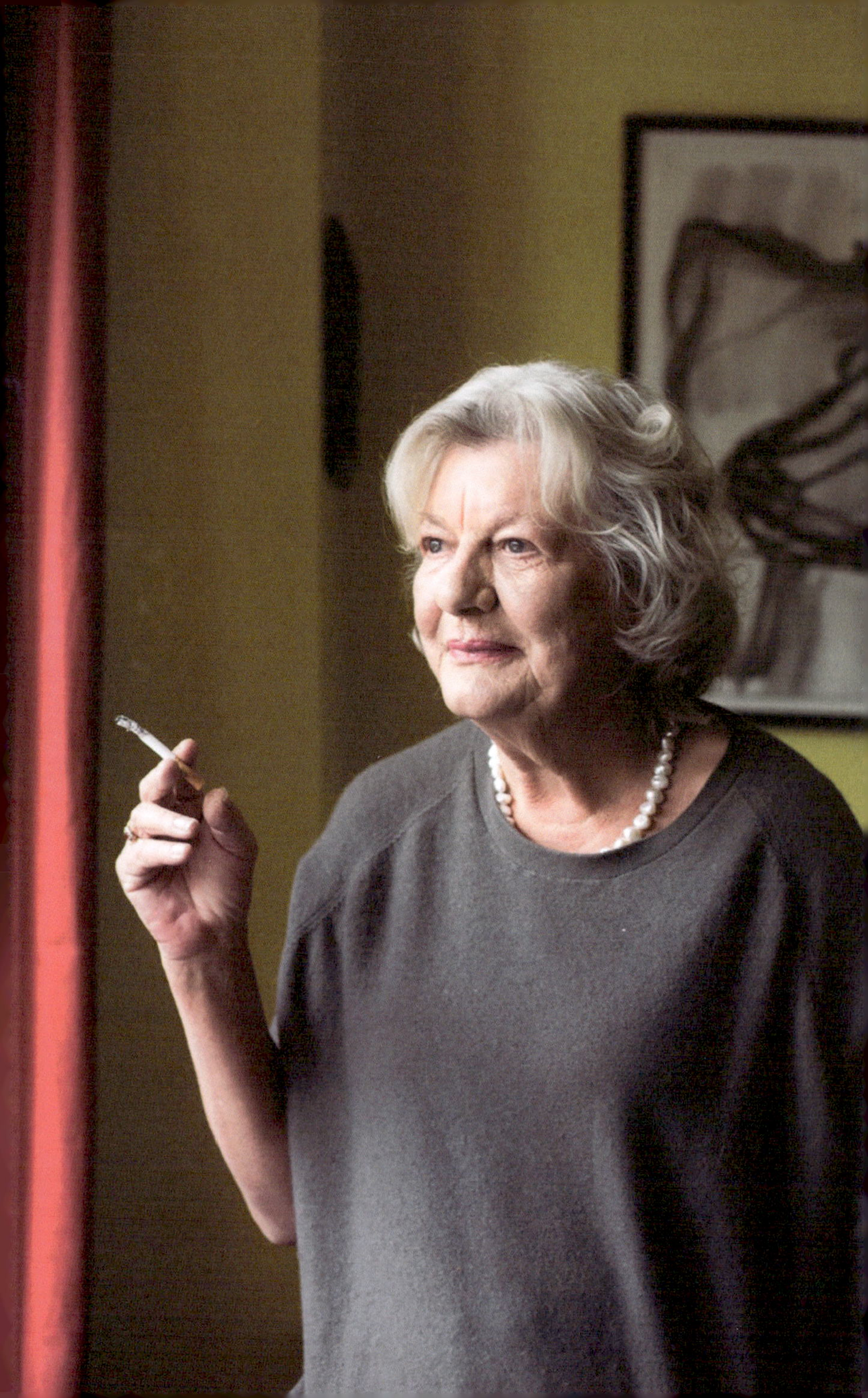

Lynn Barber

Born in 1944, Lynn Barber studied English at the University of Oxford. She began her career in journalism at *Penthouse*, and progressed to the *Independent on Sunday*, the *Observer*, the *Telegraph*, and the *Sunday Times*, as well as *Vanity Fair*. She has won six British Press Awards and has published two volumes of her celebrated interviews, *Mostly Men* and *Demon Barber*.

An Education (2009), Lynn's memoir about her schoolgirl affair with a con man, was made into an Oscar-nominated film starring Carey Mulligan in 2010, with a screenplay by Nick Hornby. *A Curious Career*, published in May 2014, continued the story of her life as a journalist and interviewer.

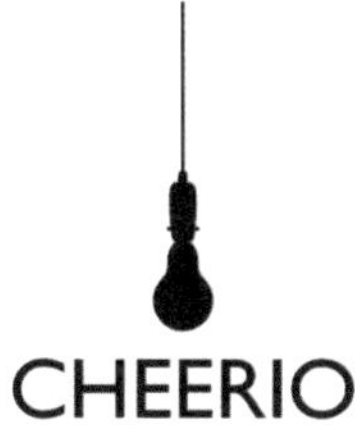

CHEERIO

First published in Great Britain in 2024 by
CHEERIO Publishing
www.cheeriopublishing.com
info@cheeriopublishing.com

Cover and book design: Mark and Keith at Mini Moderns®

Cover photograph: *Cigarette Tits (Idealized Smokers Chest II)*, 1999, Sarah Lucas. Reproduced by kind permission of Sarah Lucas.

A CIP catalogue record for this book is available from the British Library.

ISBN: 9781739440541

I am a writer, but I wish I were an artist.

Artists have more fun. They throw the best parties, they drink, they smoke, they never talk about essential vitamins or mindfulness. At school, I used to hang around the art room because that was where all the cool girls congregated at break. I longed to be one of them and hoped their talent for art would somehow rub off on me. It never did. In fact, I failed my art O-level and was told not to bother retaking it, which meant I was banished from the art room for good. Incidentally, I know of one famous artist, Marc Quinn, who failed his art O-level, but he submitted an airline sick bag full of plaster called *Night Flight*, which at least was witty, whereas I submitted a dull painting of daffodils.

This book is an account of how I've spent my life trying to get back into the art room to hang out with artists.

I am not only useless at art, but pretty ignorant about it too. I never studied art history so I am still very hazy about, say, who the Mannerists were or why Poussin is considered so important. Of course, I could read up on it but I choose not to because I have come to believe that my ignorance or (to put it more kindly) my naïvety is quite an asset. I approach art with no preconceptions whatsoever, whereas I feel that my appreciation of books is tainted by the fact that I read English Literature at university. I was taught that I had to admire George Eliot more than Jilly Cooper, for example, I still feel a twinge of guilt when I choose to read *Riders* instead of *Middlemarch*. But with art, I can respond completely spontaneously – I like it, I don't like it – with no prior feeling of what I ought to like. I think this is good. We should always listen to our gut feelings, our spontaneous responses, rather than received opinions.

My parents were not interested in art. The only picture we had on the wall at home was a Degas print of ballerinas. I liked it a lot and asked Mum where I could see some more. She said maybe in the Tate Gallery. So I took myself off to the Tate (the old one, which is now Tate Britain) and found the lovely Degas sculpture of the child ballerina in a tutu. But I was even more enchanted by the Pre-Raphaelites and looked forward to my gallery visits most Sundays to see them. (I know, I know, you're not supposed to like the Pre-Raphaelites but I still have a soft spot for them.) I bought postcards and stuck them on my bedroom wall. When I became more sophisticated (ha!), I got keen on Magritte and chortled over *Ceci n'est pas une pipe*.

It was at Oxford that I met my future husband, David. The first date he ever took me on was to the Tate Gallery. I noticed that he didn't rave about the Pre-Raphaelites, but he showed me the Blakes and the Turners and gradually began educating me. His father was head of the British Council so he'd grown up visiting galleries and reading art books. He even had a famous art teacher at Eton called Wilfred Blunt, who encouraged him to go to art school. David's parents insisted that he went to Oxford first (to read, of all things, PPP), reassuring him that he could aways paint in his spare time. Though he did this for a while, he never sold a painting and, eventually succumbing to economic necessity, wound up teaching Media Studies. But he always longed to get back to art and as soon as he could afford to take early retirement, he rented a studio in an old soap factory in Hackney (where Rachel Whiteread started), which was tragically demolished to make way for the Olympic Park. It was a wonderful, bone-freezingly cold warren of artist spaces. Many of the windows were broken. David didn't mind the cold, though – he was kept warm by his love of painting. He also went to life-drawing classes with a very good teacher, June Collier, who taught him to make his drawings bigger and bolder, less perfectionist, more dashing, which is just what he needed.

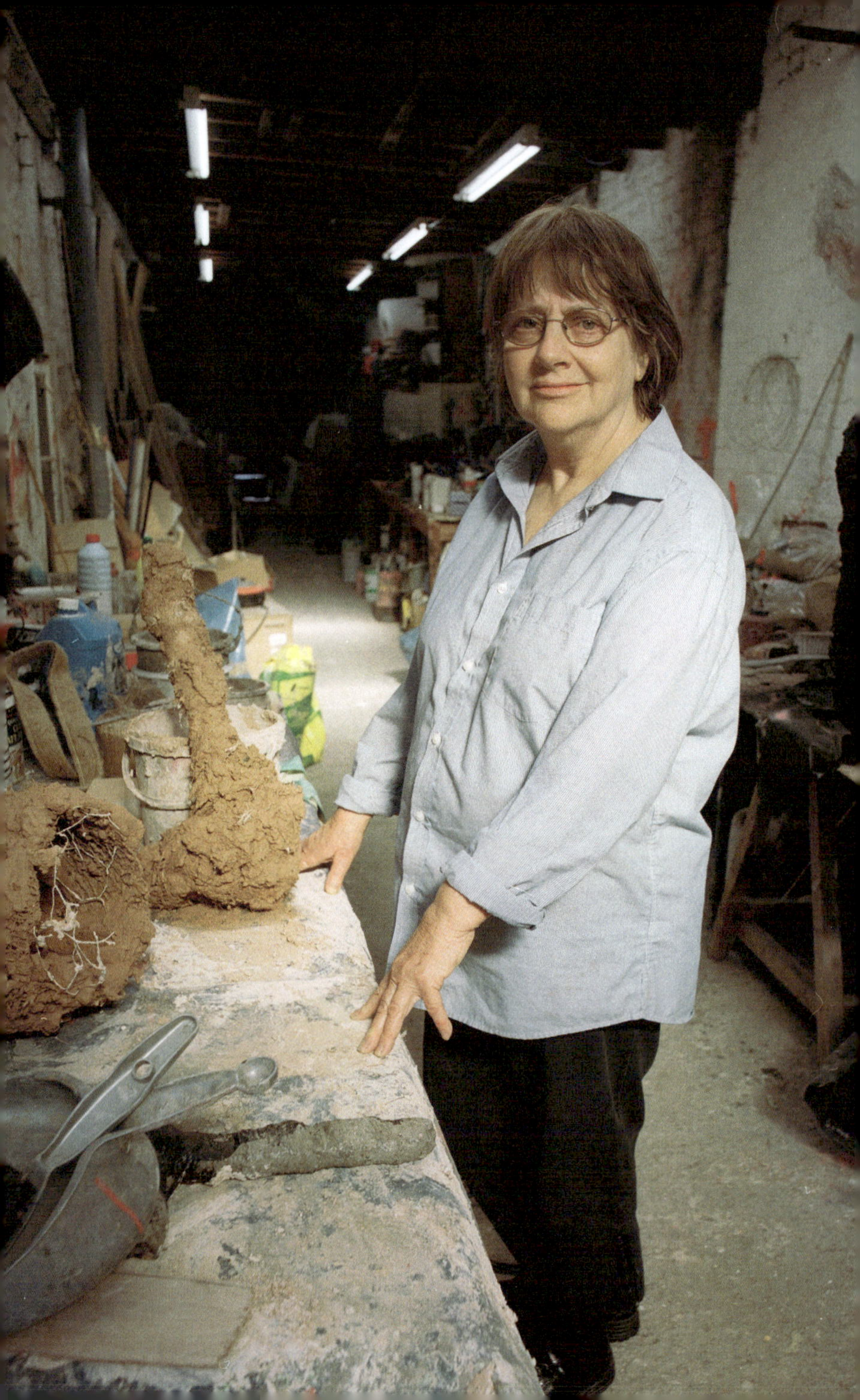

Phyllida Barlow

The first artist I ever knew, apart from David, was Phyllida Barlow. This was back in the late seventies when the children were small. We were living in Finsbury Park, and I met Phyllida through the babysitting circle. I was writing a book about Darwinism at the time and so was thrilled to learn that she was Charles Darwin's great-great-granddaughter. David was equally thrilled to learn that her husband, Fabian Peake, was the son of Mervyn Peake, whose *Gormenghast* he much admired. It was enough to form a bond.

Phyllida had five children so it never occurred to me that she might also have a career, but she mentioned one day that she was a sculptor. She claimed that she could only work at night, after the children had gone to bed. I asked if I could see her work and was led into a sort of shed beside her house which was full of stacks of wood. I kept waiting for her to show me her work, until finally I asked: 'aren't you going to show me the sculptures?' 'These are them,' she said. 'These?!' I squawked (I was hoping for marble heads – I was very naive in those days). My scorn was obvious and there was really no way of recovering, but, luckily, she had a good sense of humour, and we remained friends. We lost touch when we moved away from Finsbury Park, though I did see her many years later at a dinner for Rachel Whiteread – it turned out she had been Rachel's tutor at the Slade.

Rachel won the Turner Prize (for *House*) when she was just thirty, but Phyllida had hardly any public recognition till she was in her sixties. She was always warmly respected by other artists, especially those she had taught (Tacita Dean and Martin Creed were students of hers, as well as Rachel Whiteread), but, while they benefitted from the nineties art boom and were signed up by important galleries, her work was barely shown. She only had her first solo show in a public gallery (the Serpentine) in 2010. Very little, in fact, of her early work even survives today because it was made from bits of wood and plywood that she found in builders' skips, and she would often cannibalise it to make new sculptures.

But when, at sixty-five, she decided to retire from teaching and concentrate entirely on her own work, her career suddenly took off. Iwan Wirth, founder of the hugely influential Hauser & Wirth gallery, made the trek to Finsbury Park in 2010. His chauffeur said they must have come to the wrong address – 'I couldn't believe this was where she lived,' Wirth told the *Guardian*, 'we are in this extraordinary house, which she explained she doesn't clean ever, and this sense of children-love fills the room.' He found it 'like therapy for a Swiss soul. This is the opposite of what we were brought up with. It was love at first sight.'

So, he signed her to Hauser & Wirth and set about promoting her career. He said she should make larger work, and fixed her up with a hangar-sized studio and a team of assistants. Overnight everyone wanted to have a Phyllida Barlow exhibition, and in 2017 she was chosen to represent Britain at the Venice Biennale.

At that time I was briefly a TV presenter on BBC2's *Artsnight*, so I went back to Finsbury Park to interview Phyllida. The house looked exactly the same (I suspect there were even some of the same pickle jars on the kitchen table) but the old woodshed had been transformed into a drawing studio and Fabian now had a separate studio at the end of the garden. Phyllida showed me some of her drawings (she had always drawn every day), then we drove to her manufacturing studio, a vast hangar in a business park behind Alexandra Palace, where teams of

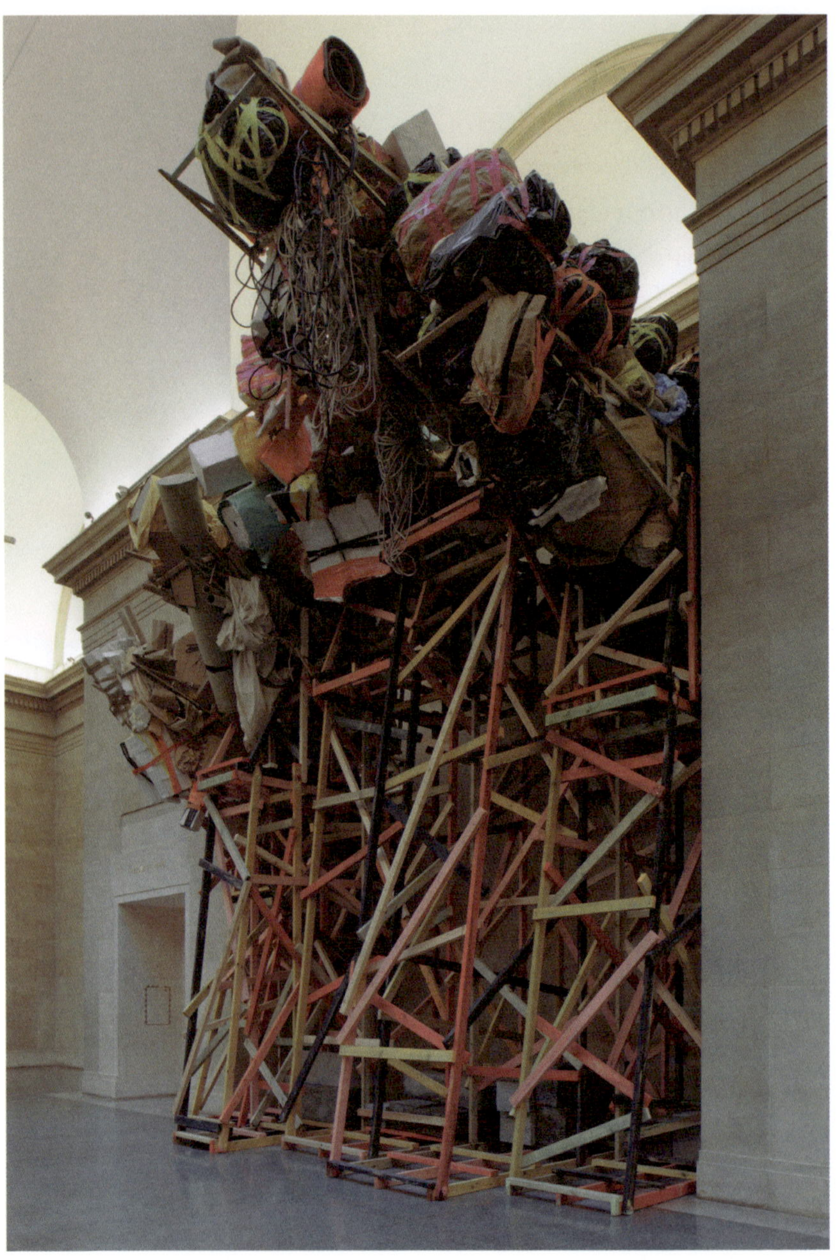

assistants were building huge structures for the Biennale. It was here that I finally 'got' her work (about time!) and realised what makes it so intriguing. It's the feeling of precariousness, as if the whole edifice has just been thrown together out of bits of old wood and scrap and could easily collapse at any moment. She told me that her old Chelsea art school tutor George Fullard had taught that 'a sculpture that falls over or breaks is just as exciting as one that reveals itself perfectly formed'. The world saw the truth of this when we all watched the statue of Gaddafi being toppled. Her Biennale exhibition was well received, and she was made a Dame in 2021. But then she died of a stroke in 2023. I'm glad I met her through the Finsbury Park babysitting circle, but I fiercely regret that I was so slow to appreciate her work.

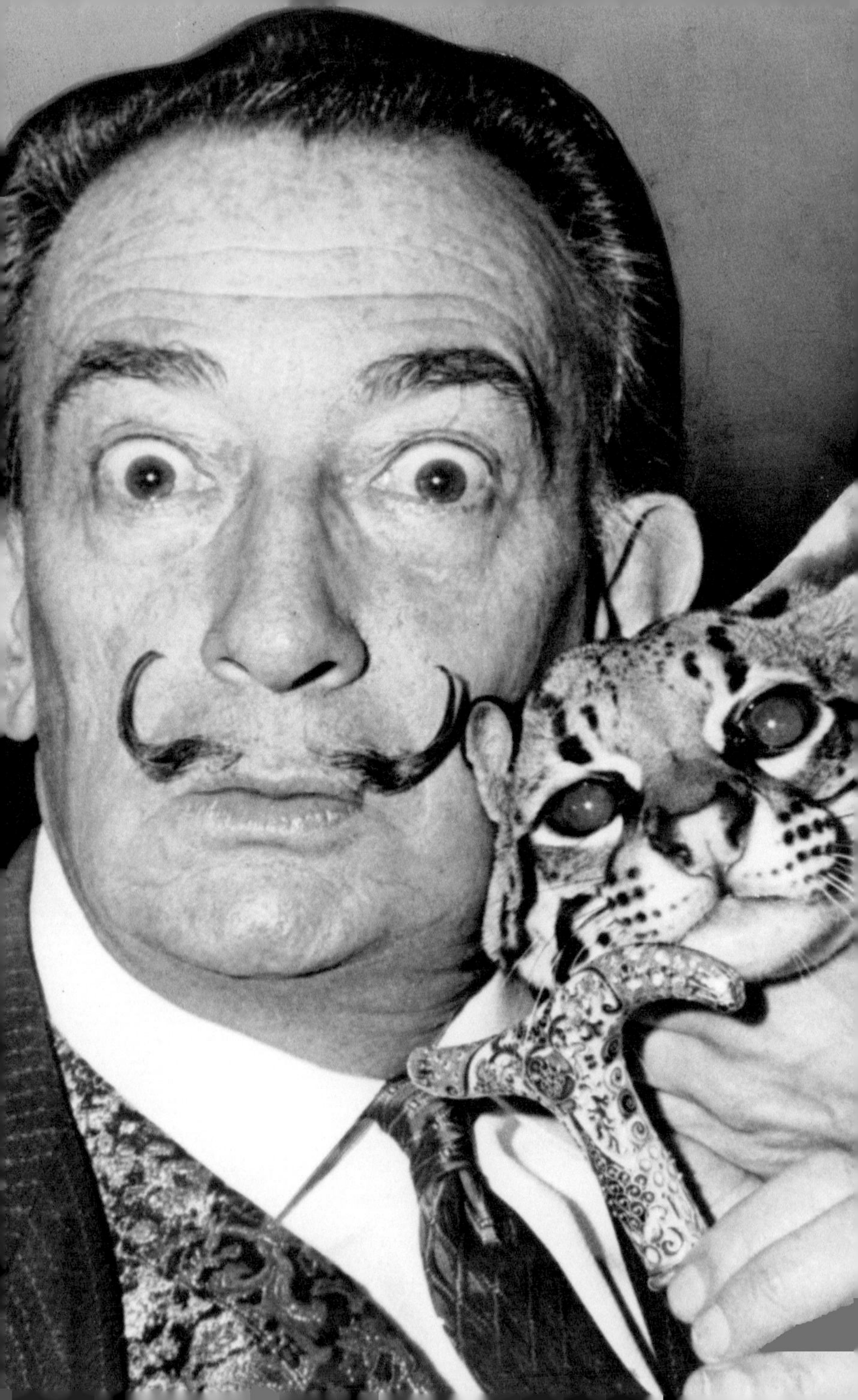

Salvador Dalí

In 1969, when I was working for *Penthouse* magazine, I was invited to interview Salvador Dalí. Bob Guccione, the magazine's founder, asked if I spoke French, and I said yes (not strictly true). He said he wanted me to go to Paris and interview Dalí at the Hotel Meurice. I had never flown anywhere alone before, and I'd certainly never been to a really grand hotel, so it was all wildly exciting. I was met in the lobby by a short, dapper Irishman who introduced himself as Captain Moore, Dalí's secretary, and led me down miles of corridor to the artist's suite. He advised me to address Dalí as 'Maître' which came quite naturally when I met him – he was so tall, so old, so grand and so exotic-looking with his wonderful, waxed moustache.

Guccione had told me to ask Dalí about sex, which of course I did, and Dalí immediately started enthusing about masturbation – 'Zee painters are always zee big masturbators – nevaire make love, only watch, and sometimes masturbation!' He told me that 'Every big artist, every important people – Michelangelo, Leonardo, Napoleon – is impotent and this is good. Because if you work too well with your sex, you never produce nozzing. Only childs. But for artist, le libido and le sexual instincts sublimate in the artistic creation.'

Dalí seemed to enjoy being interviewed, and we were soon joined by his considerable retinue, all earwigging. But each time Dalí's wife Gala walked in, everyone drifted away – they were all terrified of her. Captain Moore told me that Dalí and Gala always lunched alone, but that I could join him, his fiancée, and – a considerable bonus – Dalí's ocelot who seemed quite at home in the Meurice dining room. When we'd finished, Captain Moore suggested that I might like to join him and his fiancé for a threesome at their flat. This was a familiar occupational hazard of working for *Penthouse* – everyone assumed I liked threesomes – and I gave my familiar answer: that I'd love to, but it was the wrong time of the month.

I was meant to join Dalí for tea, but a Japanese journalist was already battering him with questions, and then a troupe of actors, Julian Beck's Living Theatre, walked in and fell on the drinks trolley. Dalí said we should talk again in the morning but, as I explained, I had to catch a plane back to London and had nowhere to stay in Paris. Dalí told Captain Moore to get me a room at the Meurice.

So, there I stayed for three days, interviewing Dalí every morning and going to parties in his suite every evening. It was only when Gala started giving me the evil eye that Dalí said he thought we'd done enough interviewing. He gave me a wonderful goodbye present – a conical hat covered with wax flowers and butterflies that he had designed for Gala to wear to a fancy dress ball in the 1930s. Years later, when a Stuttgart museum asked to borrow it for an exhibition, they insured it for £15,000.

Meeting Dalí gave me a strong desire to interview as many artists as possible, but in those days, artists very rarely came up on the media radar. It must be hard for younger readers to appreciate just how hostile Britain was to contemporary art right up until the nineties. Newspapers still ran cartoons about torsos with holes in (Henry Moore) or faces with two noses (Picasso). Many people who claimed to be art lovers only went to Monet shows at the Royal Academy. There had been a small spark of interest with the arrival of David Hockney in the sixties – even philistines liked his portrait of *Mr and Mrs Clark and Percy* – but affection waned when he moved to the States and became more abstract. Abstract art was obviously beyond the pale. I remember the enormous hoo-ha when the Tate bought Carl Andre's *Equivalent VIII* in 1974. The media went berserk at the idea of spending taxpayers' money on a pile of firebricks.

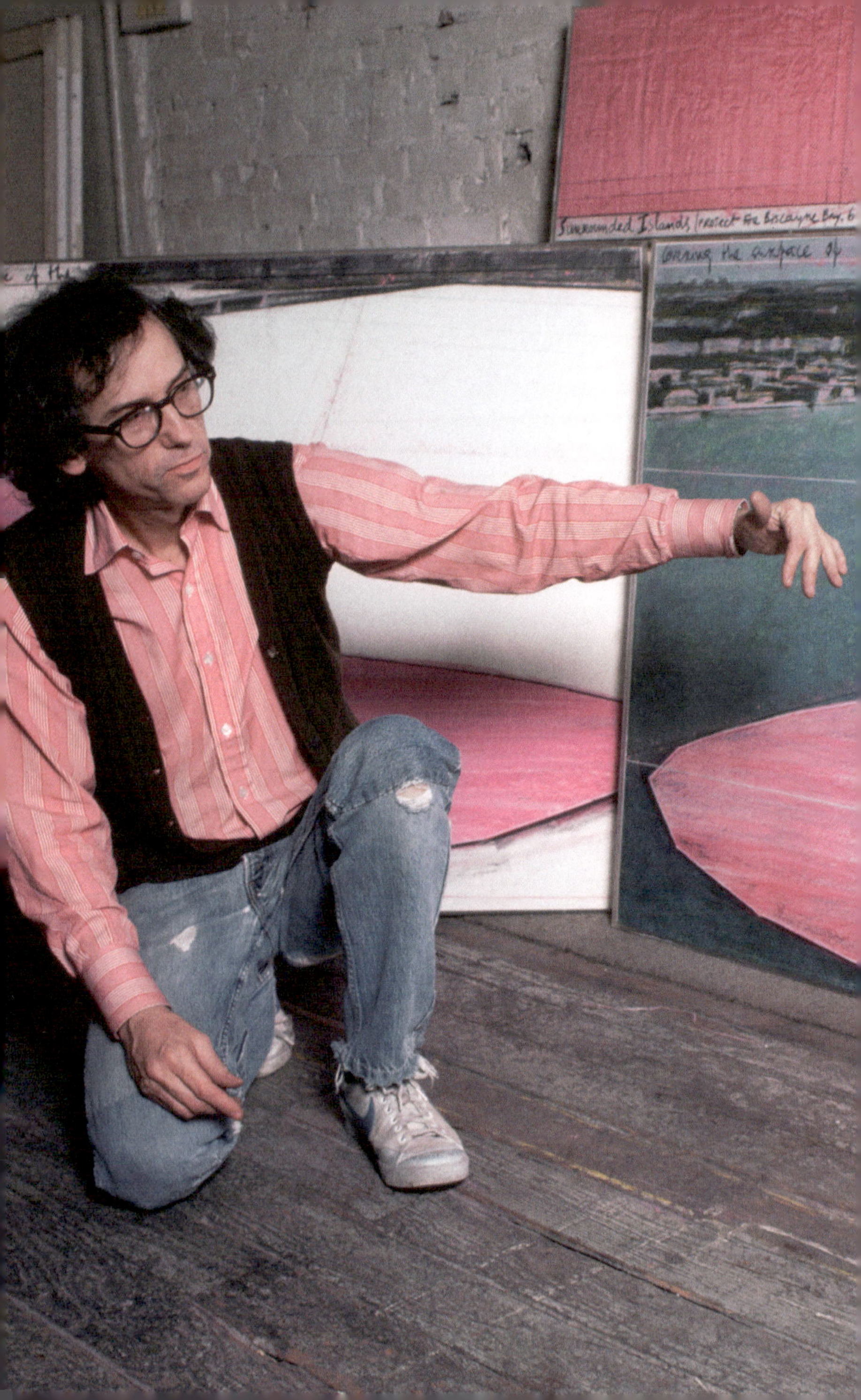
Surrounded Islands (Project for Biscayne Bay, 6
covering the surface of
of the

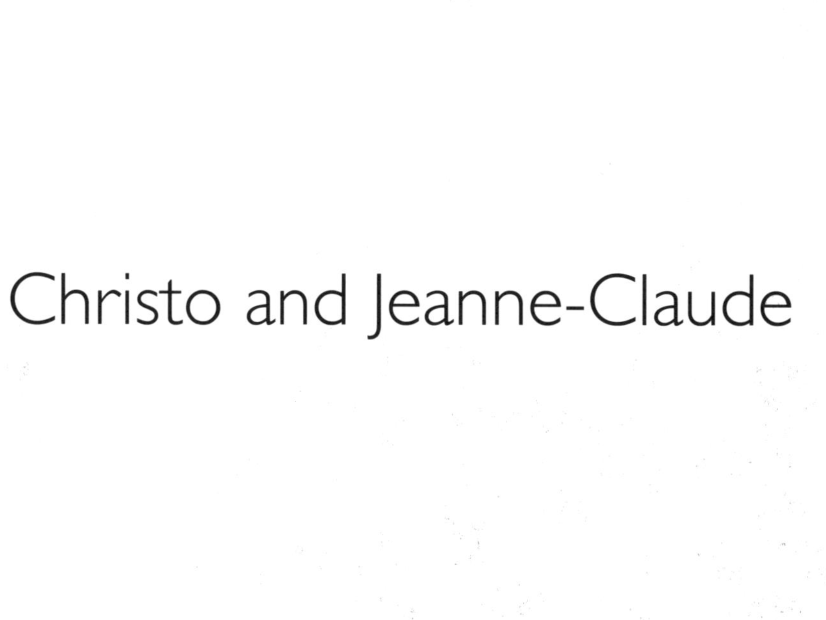

Christo and Jeanne-Claude

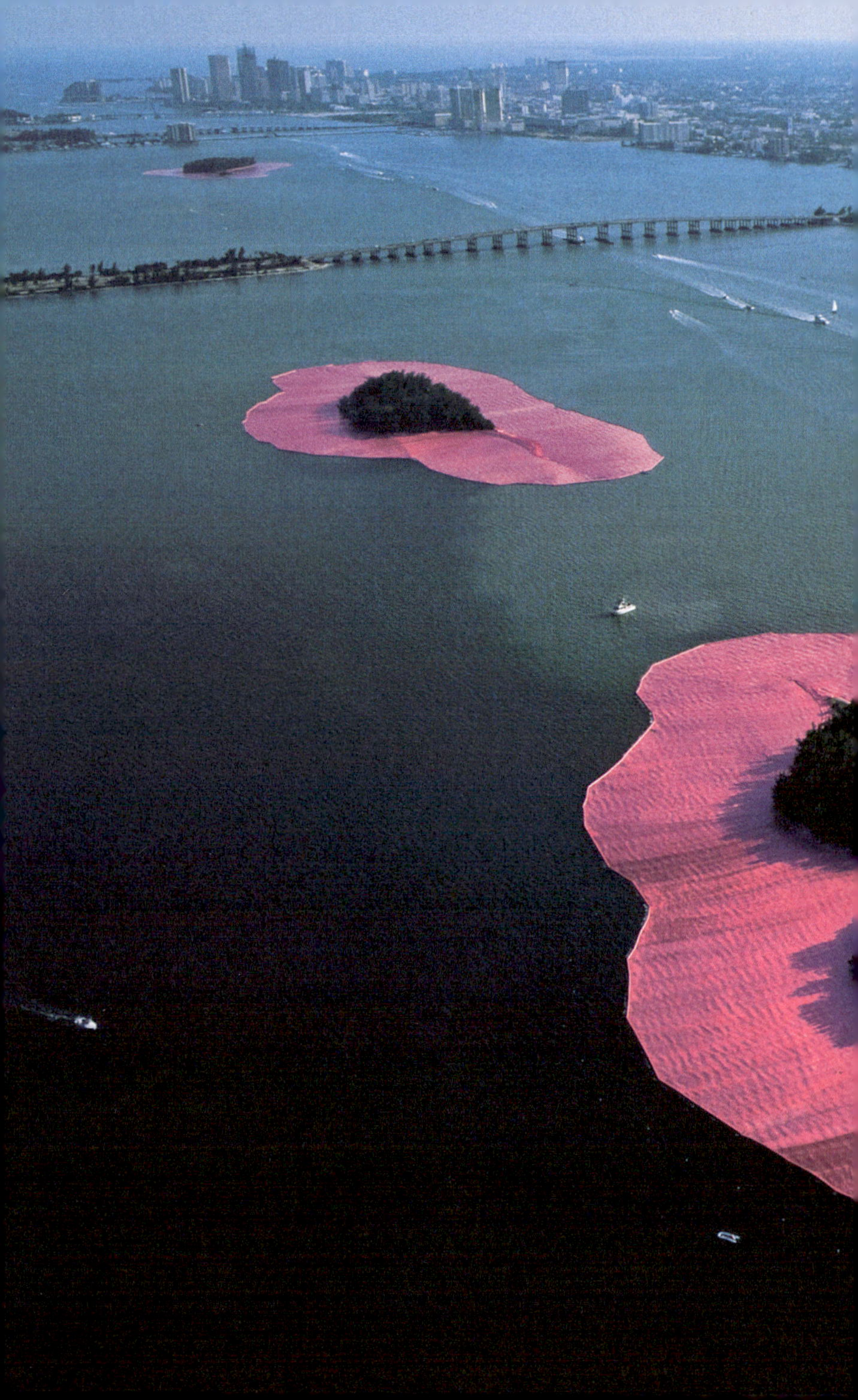

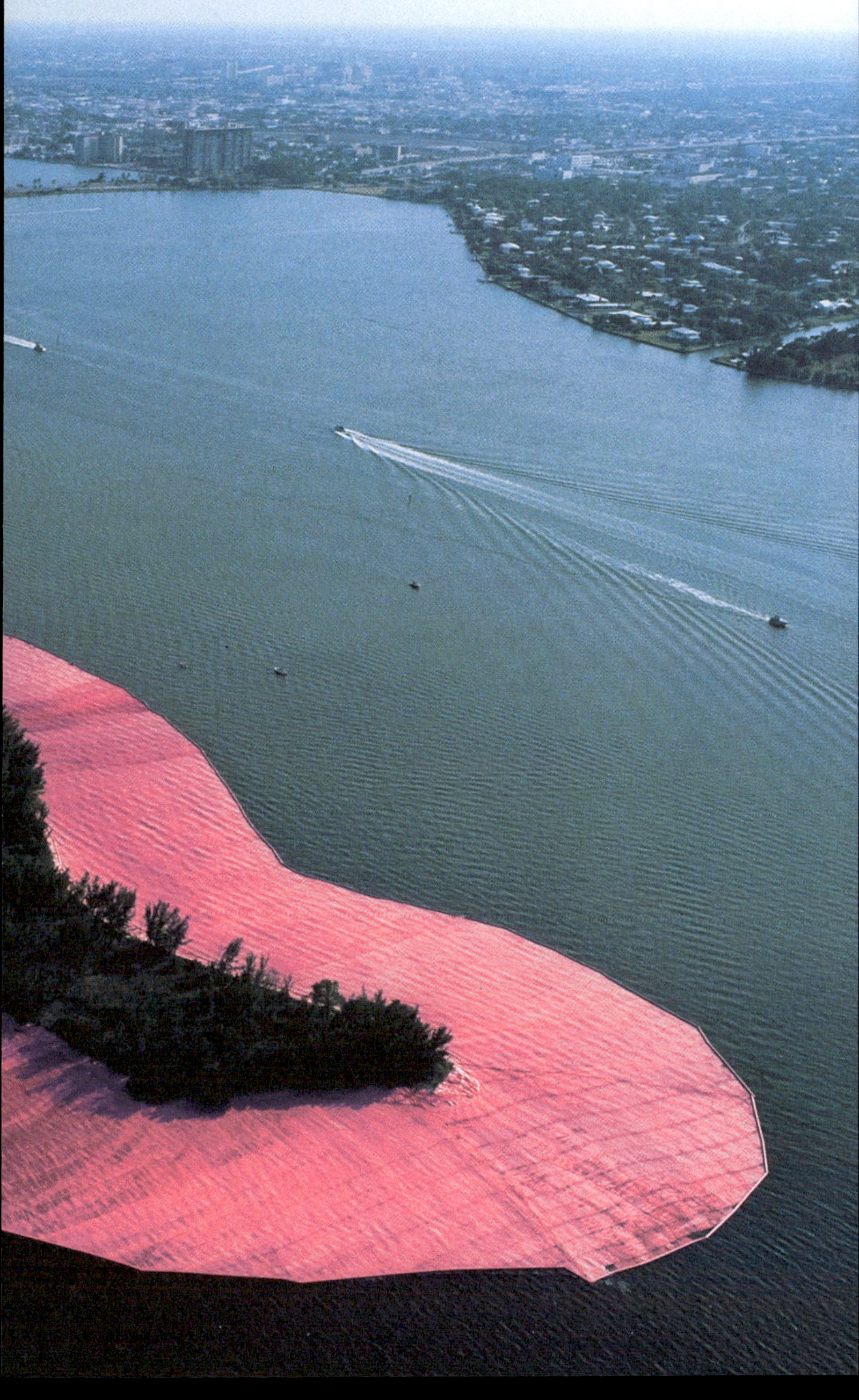

After *Penthouse*, I went to the *Sunday Express Magazine* but only interviewed two artists in the seven years I worked there and one of them, I regret to say, was Rolf Harris. The other was Christo, which came about for an odd reason. My editor, Ron Hall, had no interest in art but happened to fly over Miami in 1983 and saw Christo's *Surrounded Islands* from the plane. These were eleven islands in Biscayne Bay that Christo had surrounded with floating pink polypropylene skirts and Ron was impressed – he liked the idea of art you could see from a plane. He suggested that I interview Christo if he ever came to Europe. And luckily for me, two years later, Christo came to Paris to wrap the Pont Neuf. I thought the Pont Neuf was one of his least successful projects – the wrapping was a sort of dull beige and looked like building works, but Christo and Jeanne-Claude, his

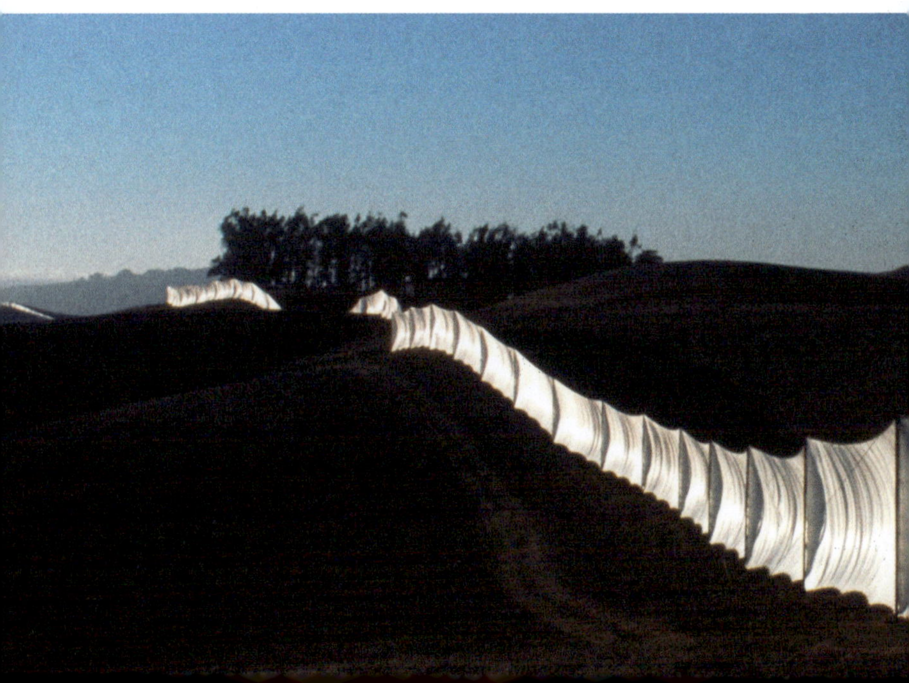

wife and creative partner, were terrific.

They both relished all the technical problems, the planning applications, the health and safety checks, the town hall meetings as a way of getting communities engaged with the work. They financed their projects themselves, from the sale of preliminary drawings and sketches, so they did not have to kowtow to any sponsors or patrons. And some of their projects – the *Running Fence*, the *Wrapped Reichstag*, the *Surrounded Islands* – were truly great.

Many years later, in 2018, my elder daughter Rosie was working for the Serpentine Gallery, and met Christo when he came to create his *Mastaba* – an installation of 7,506 oil barrels on a raft in the Serpentine lake. She said he was tremendous fun but by then, sadly, Jeanne-Claude had died.

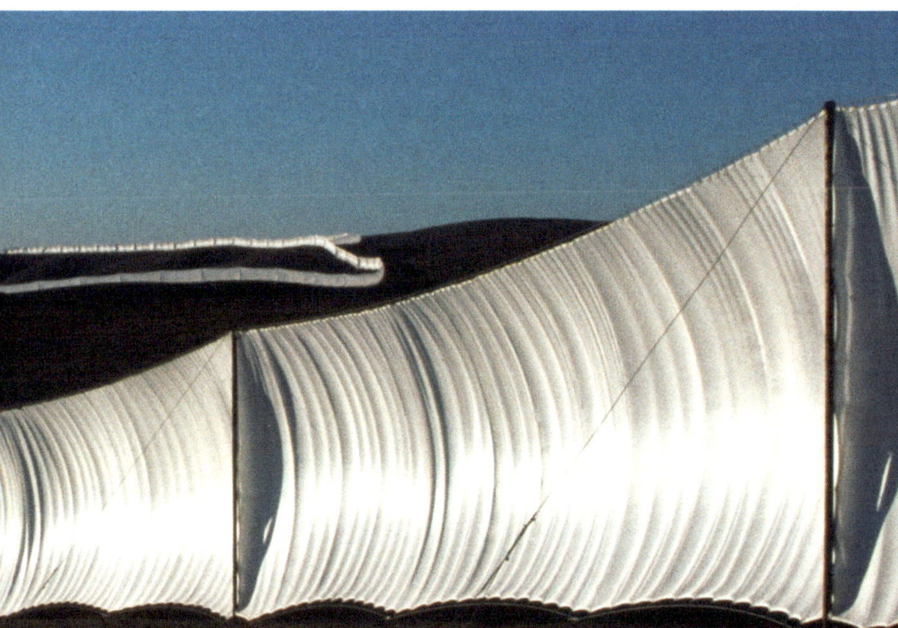

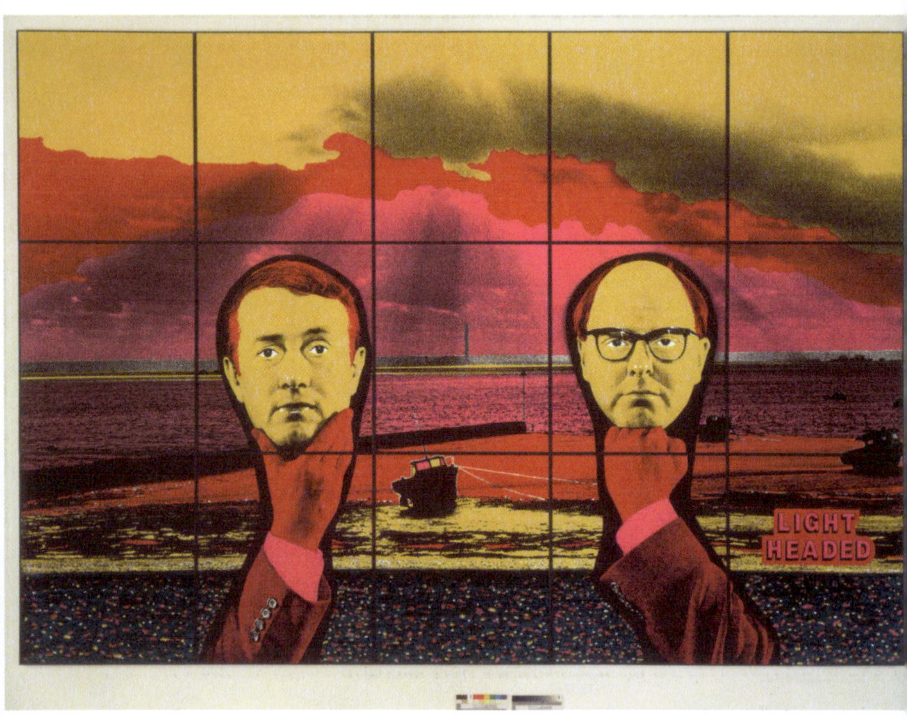

LIGHT
HEADED

Gilbert and George

In 1990, I moved to the *Independent on Sunday* which was generally more friendly to the idea of interviewing artists. In one of the first issues, I interviewed Gilbert and George at their home in Fournier Street. Of course, they gave their usual carefully crafted double act, speaking in unison, or finishing each other's sentences. I got the impression that George was the 'enforcer', and that Gilbert would probably have spoken more freely if George wasn't there. And George was annoyed when I told him I knew he was married – I knew someone who knew his wife. I also managed to track down his early art teacher in Totnes who said he was a lovely boy: he used to babysit their children.

Gilbert and George were useful pioneers for the art scene generally in that they moved to Spitalfields back in 1968, when the area was completely derelict. This brought salvation to Sandra Esquilant, licensee of the Golden Heart on Commercial Road. She remembers how glad she was to see them come in 'suited and booted' (i.e. properly attired) when her pub was becoming hopelessly depopulated, and how they cheered the place up by bringing in their assistants, including the Chapman brothers.

Later, Tracey Emin would move into Spitalfields, and the Golden Heart would become the YBAs' pub of choice and almost every art party would begin or end there. Sandra Esquilant became good friends with Tracey Emin, but she remains most grateful to Gilbert and George: '*They were fantastic. They are fantastic.*'

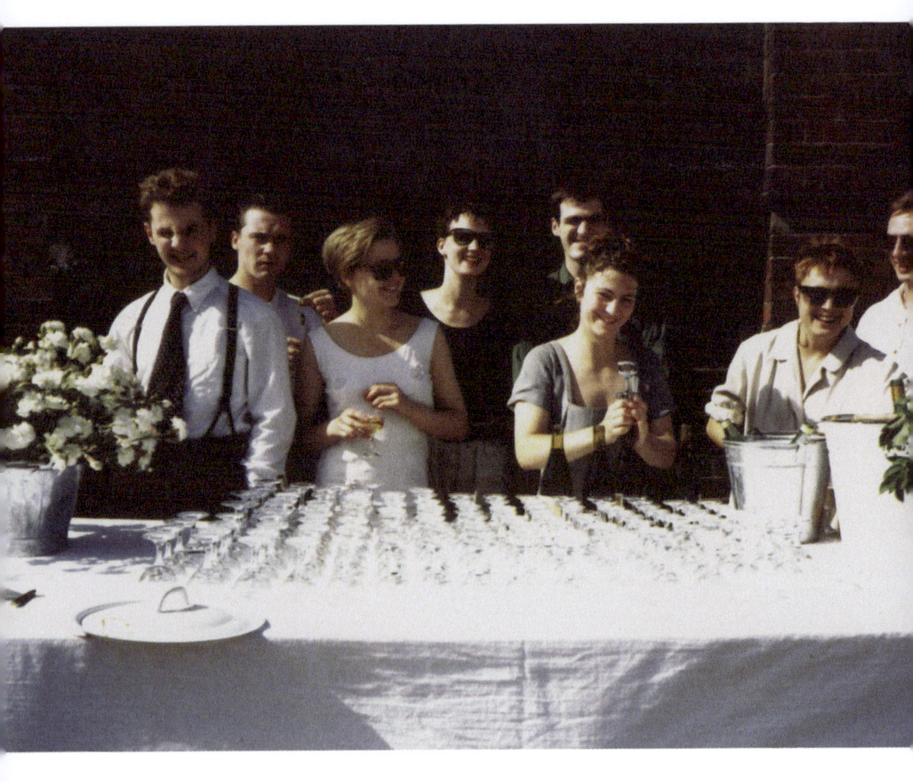

Enter the YBAs

I moved to the *Observer* just when the contemporary art scene was beginning to take off, thanks to the *Sensation* show in 1997. This only came about by chance: the Royal Academy's planned blockbuster exhibition was cancelled at the last minute and the curator Norman Rosenthal had to rustle something up very quickly. He had the brilliant idea of asking Charles Saatchi if he could borrow his collection, which he'd been showing at his own gallery in Boundary Road, St John's Wood. It proved to be, indeed, a sensation, provoking endless controversy. Several Academicians, including my friend Gillian Ayres, resigned in fury at the Myra Hindley painting by Marcus Harvey.

The effect of the *Sensation* show was that the media were suddenly interested in all these new Young British Artists, and the *Observer* sent me to interview many of them: Tracey Emin, Damien Hirst, Sarah Lucas, Rachel Whiteread, Gary Hume, Marc Quinn, Jake and Dinos Chapman. I enjoyed interviewing artists a million times more than actors, who were the normal bread and butter of celebrity interviews, so I made it a rule that if I interviewed half a dozen actors on the trot, I should be allowed to choose an artist as my next target.

In those early days, when the YBAs were new and largely unknown (and of course this was before Wikipedia or Google), I was often just trying to get basic biographical information – where they grew up, what art schools they went to, who or what had influenced them. The last thing on earth I wanted to hear was their theory of art or the sort of bollocks they put in art catalogues.

But it was often an uphill task.

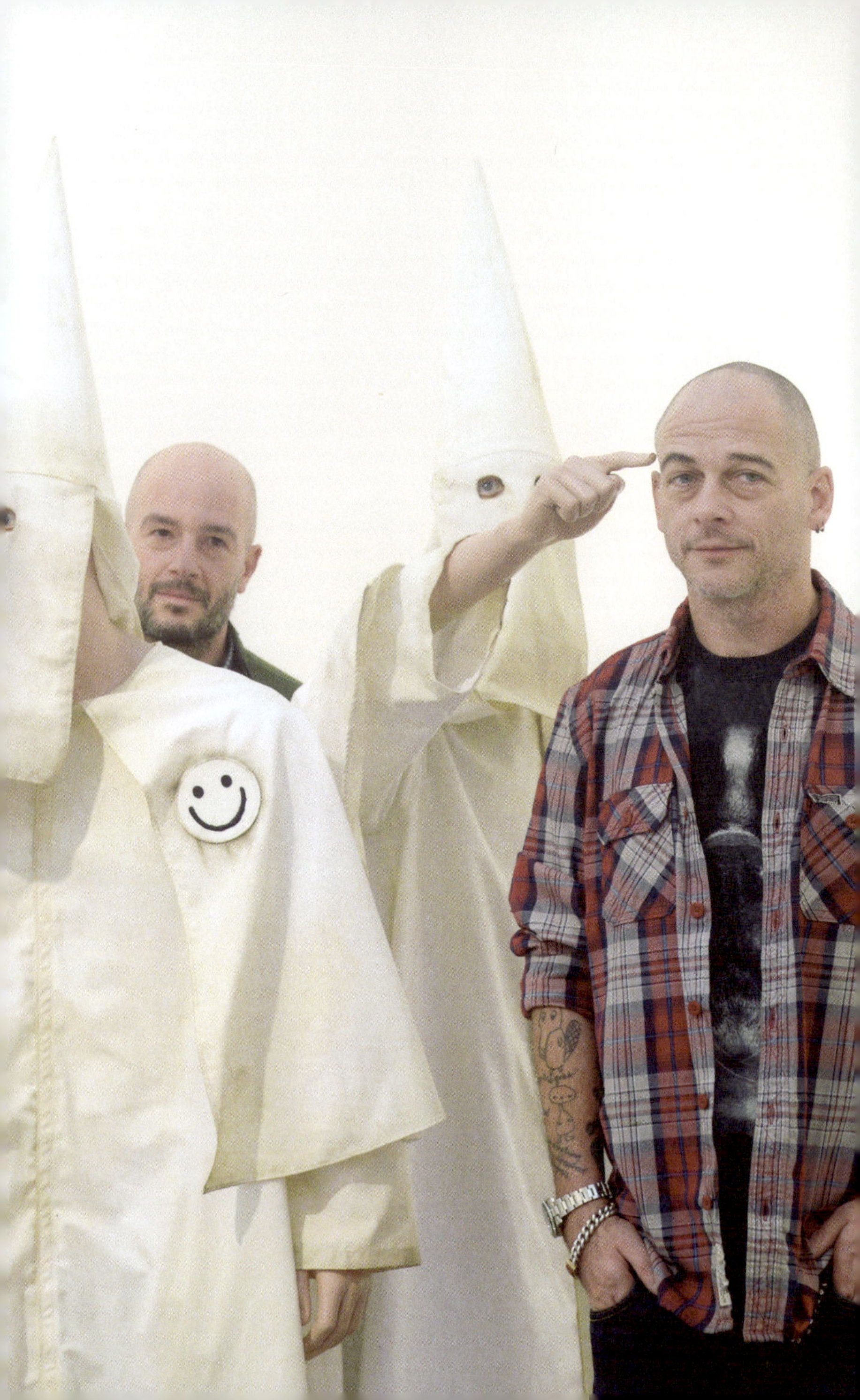

The Chapman Brothers

The Chapman Brothers were particularly difficult. They claimed that they couldn't even remember their childhoods and that it was not relevant to their art in any way. Yet one of their first major works, produced in 1994, was called *Mummy and Daddy Chapman*, in which Mummy had a nasty rash of penises all over her body. Daddy had a similar rash of anal sphincters.

Not a happy childhood then?

They immediately started explaining, almost in unison, that there were hundreds of Mr and Mrs Chapmans in the phone book, and the work was in no way related to their parents.

I chose to interview the Chapman Brothers because I admired their work, but unfortunately, they hated me more or less on sight. Jake kept telling me I was 'bourgeois', which he seemed to regard as a deadly sin. He said their work was political and intended to shock, alienate, and undermine the viewer. He once memorably said in an interview that he wanted: 'to rub salt into your inferiority complex, smash your ego in the face, gouge your eyes from their sockets and piss in the empty holes.'

I went to see them at their freezing cold studio off the Peckham Road where the work in progress was a Nazi death camp, twenty-eight feet long, which would be shaped like a swastika, with hundreds of bodies strewn about. They had bought the bodies from a military modelling catalogue, but they came as separate arms and legs and torsos which had to be stuck together. It was as fiddly as building a cathedral out of matchsticks. (They told me that they bought the penises for their *Fuck Face* figures from Ann Summers shops, which must have been easier.)

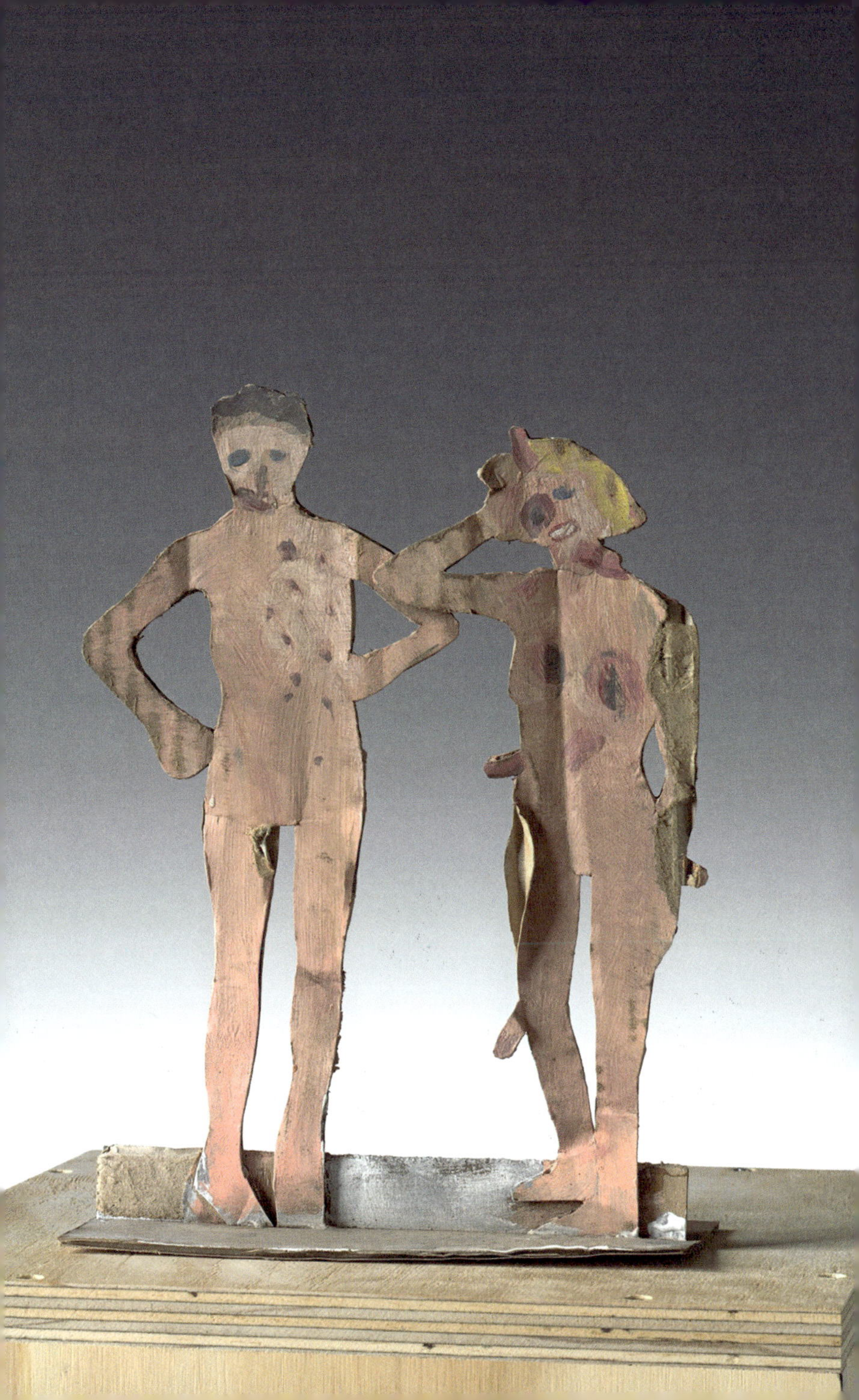

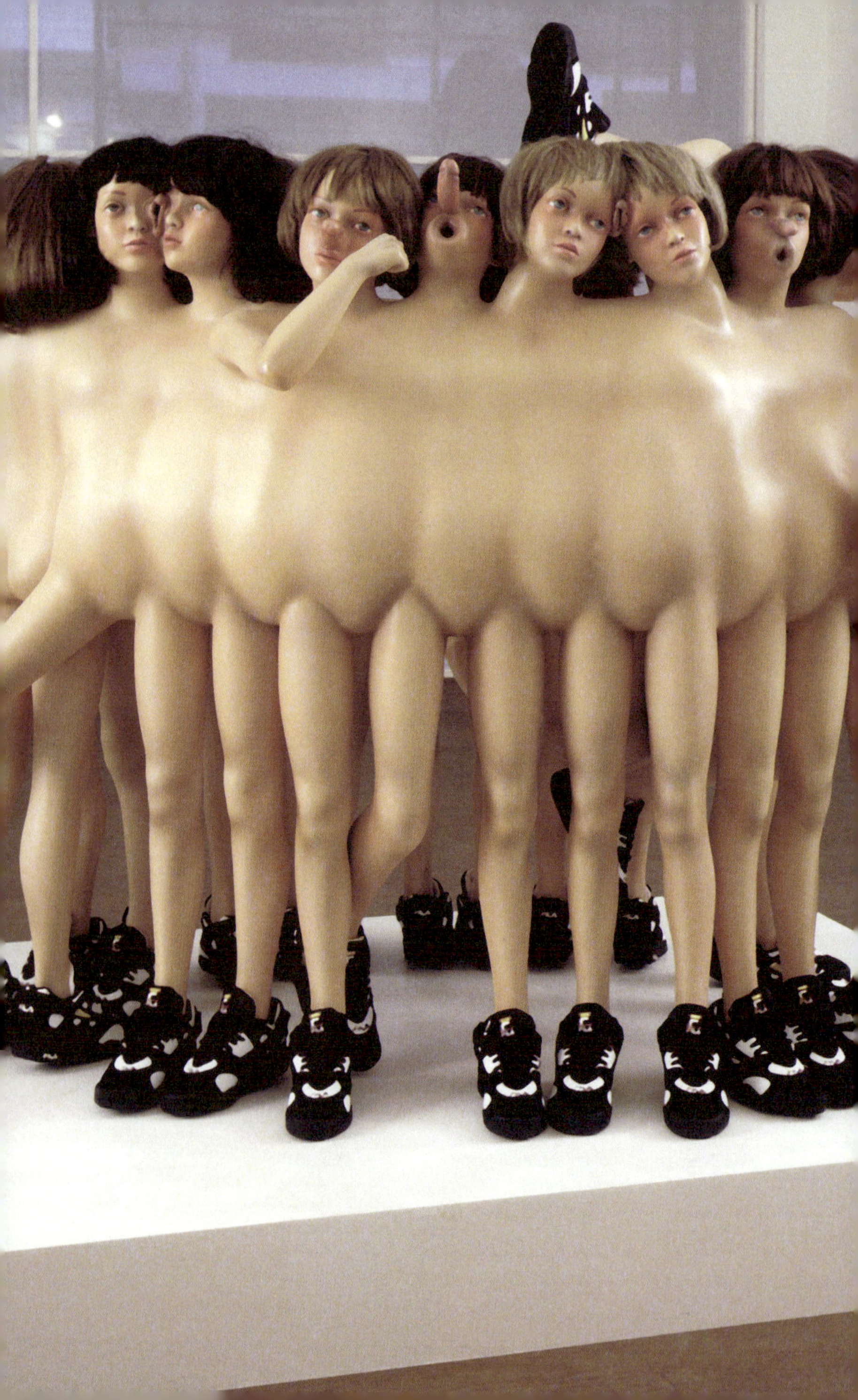

It was too cold to talk in the studio, so we adjourned to a nearby McDonald's where Jake went on lecturing me about their artistic aims: 'Our work is intensely strategic, intensely non-human, intensely cruel.' There were hours of this stuff and, inevitably, my attention wandered. I noticed that one of Dinos's hands was slightly, and the other markedly, deformed with the fingers pulled back as if hanging from a window ledge. Eventually I asked what was wrong with his hands. 'Was it congenital? He said, 'that's irrelevant,' but I replied that 'surely, it's as relevant as possible, given that you make works based on genetic mutations?' Jake went through the roof. 'How can you be so *dumb* as to ask questions like that?'

We parted on bad terms but met up again at a party at Sadie Coles HQ in Heddon Street, which moved on to the Zinc Bar. In the few yards between Sadie's gallery and the bar, Jake did a deal with one of the party guests to swap a set of their new Goya etchings for a motorbike. Dinos was furious and, by the time we sat down, they were already squabbling. Jake started lecturing me again about how stupid and bourgeois I was, and eventually I freaked and seized Dinos's hand and said, 'You have got to tell me about it! You make works about genetic mutation for chrissake!' Jake stormed out but I was still hanging on to Dinos's hand. He started talking very quietly and urgently: 'What you're doing is fascist! If someone isn't entirely, totally, absolutely fucking normal by your rules, then they're abnormal. I had arthritis. The end. We make sculptures. The end. We are interesting because of what we do now, not because of what we were when we were kids.'

When my interview was published in the *Observer Magazine*, I

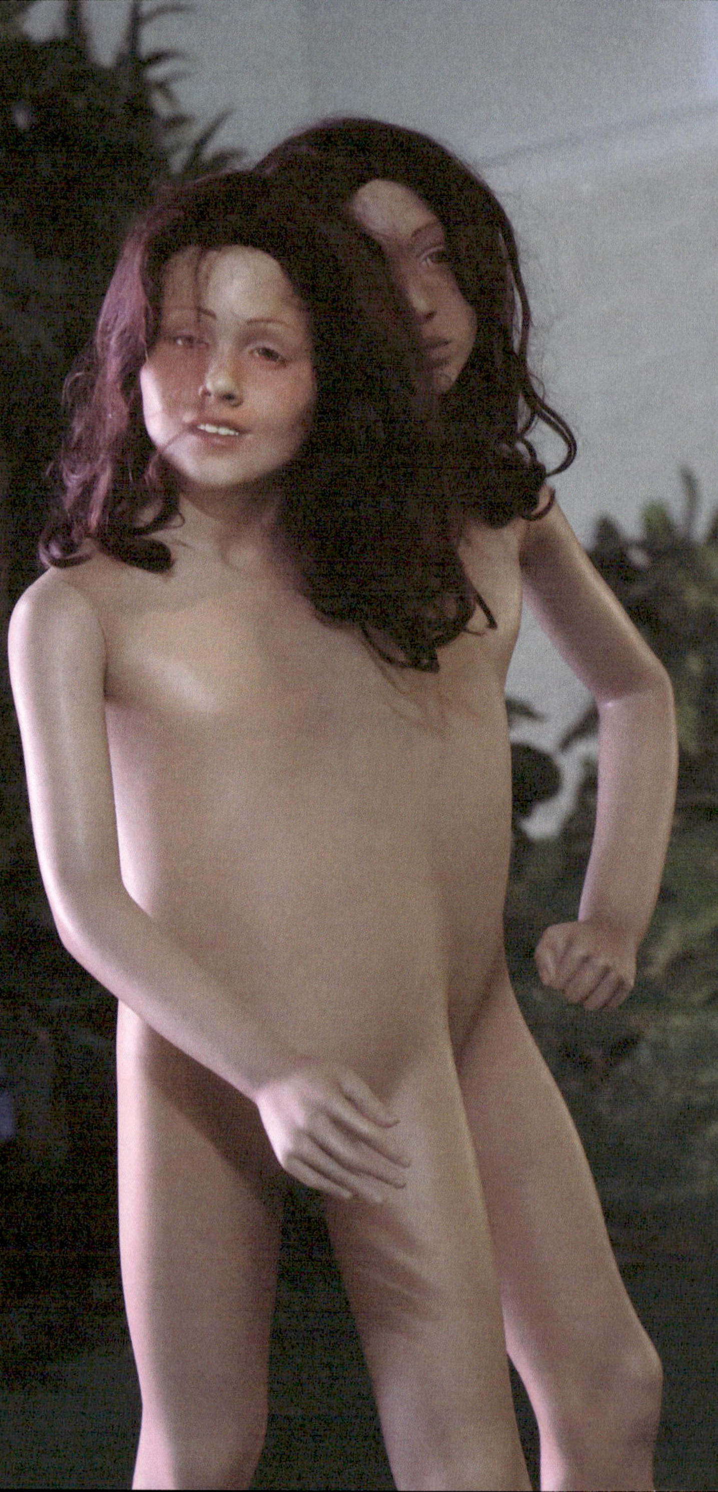

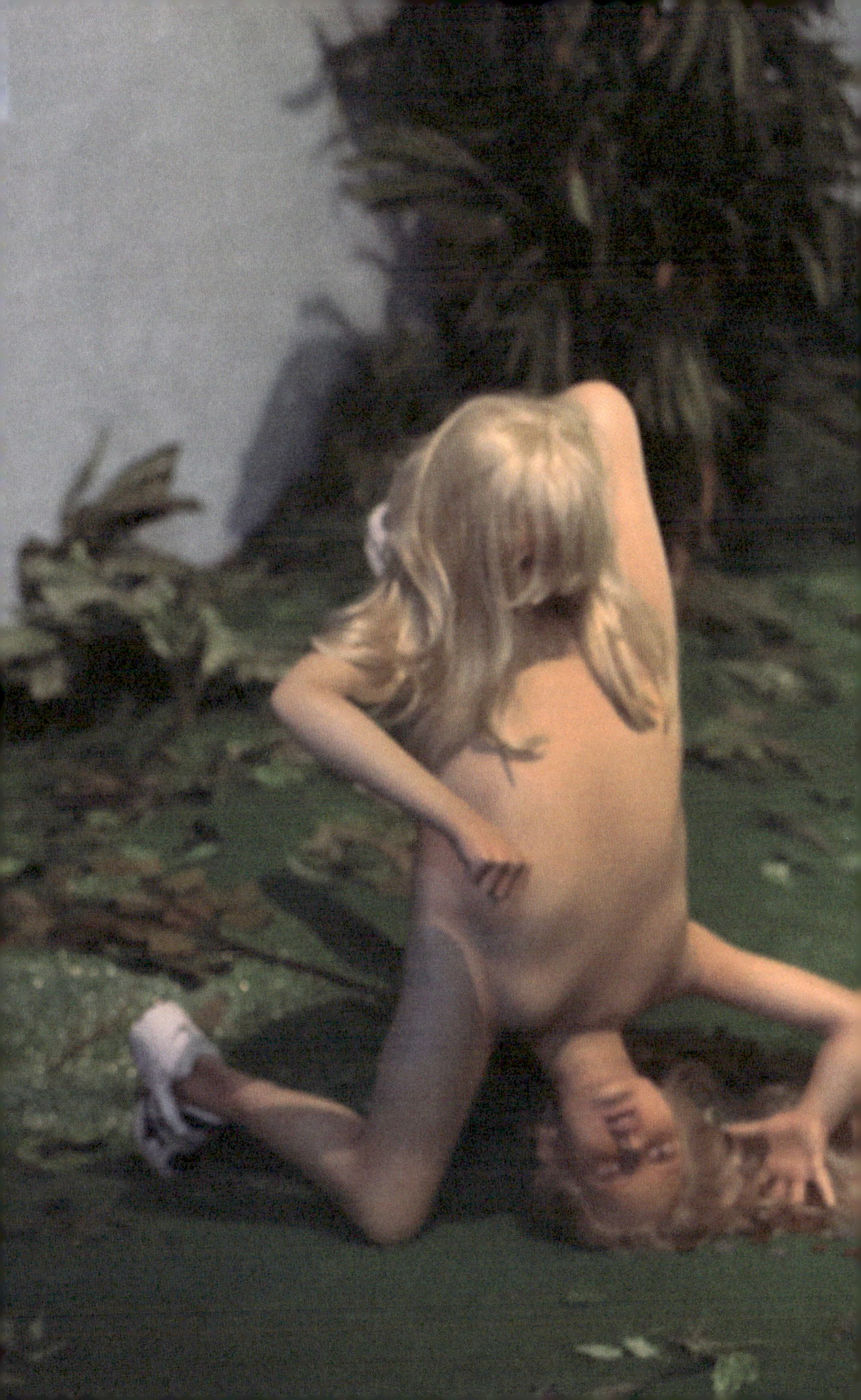

got a message that the Chapman Brothers would kill me if they ever saw me again. I took this threat sufficiently seriously to make a point of avoiding them at parties, though Dinos once came up to me and said he enjoyed an article I'd written about birdwatching in Trinidad. And, last summer, I ran into Jake at Tracey Emin's exhibition in Margate, and he said it was great to see me. He emailed me afterwards, as follows:

Dear Lynn,

I'm not sure if the cosmos could ever have anticipated the event of us bumping into each other at a Tracey Emin exhibition in Margate but it was very nice speaking with you and reminded me that I should have by now cleared up the bad feeling caused by me in our last encounter.

Covid precipitated a huge change in which I finally decided to work alone (new solo career at 55 – woodcarving in the Cotswolds no less) and after two years of estrangement from my brother, I'm now happily liberated from the defensiveness that characterised elements of our collaboration – to which you fell foul some years ago.

I owed you an apology then, but hope you'll accept it now. My diehard defence of Dinos and his childhood illness is/was so embedded in my DNA that only recently have I realised how myopic and unnecessary it was. You certainly didn't deserve my frustration and even less my anger, and so I apologise deeply. It was lovely to see you, and especially at Tracey's amazing show (since it's also been amazing reconnecting with her). Hope you're well and be good to see you soon.

Jake Xx

So now I am friends with Jake Chapman. In fact, I emailed him earlier this year to ask why he didn't come to the opening of Tracey's new studios, and he said he was doing a sea survival course in Devon. Why on earth? He said he was planning to row across the Atlantic.

I warmly hope he survives.

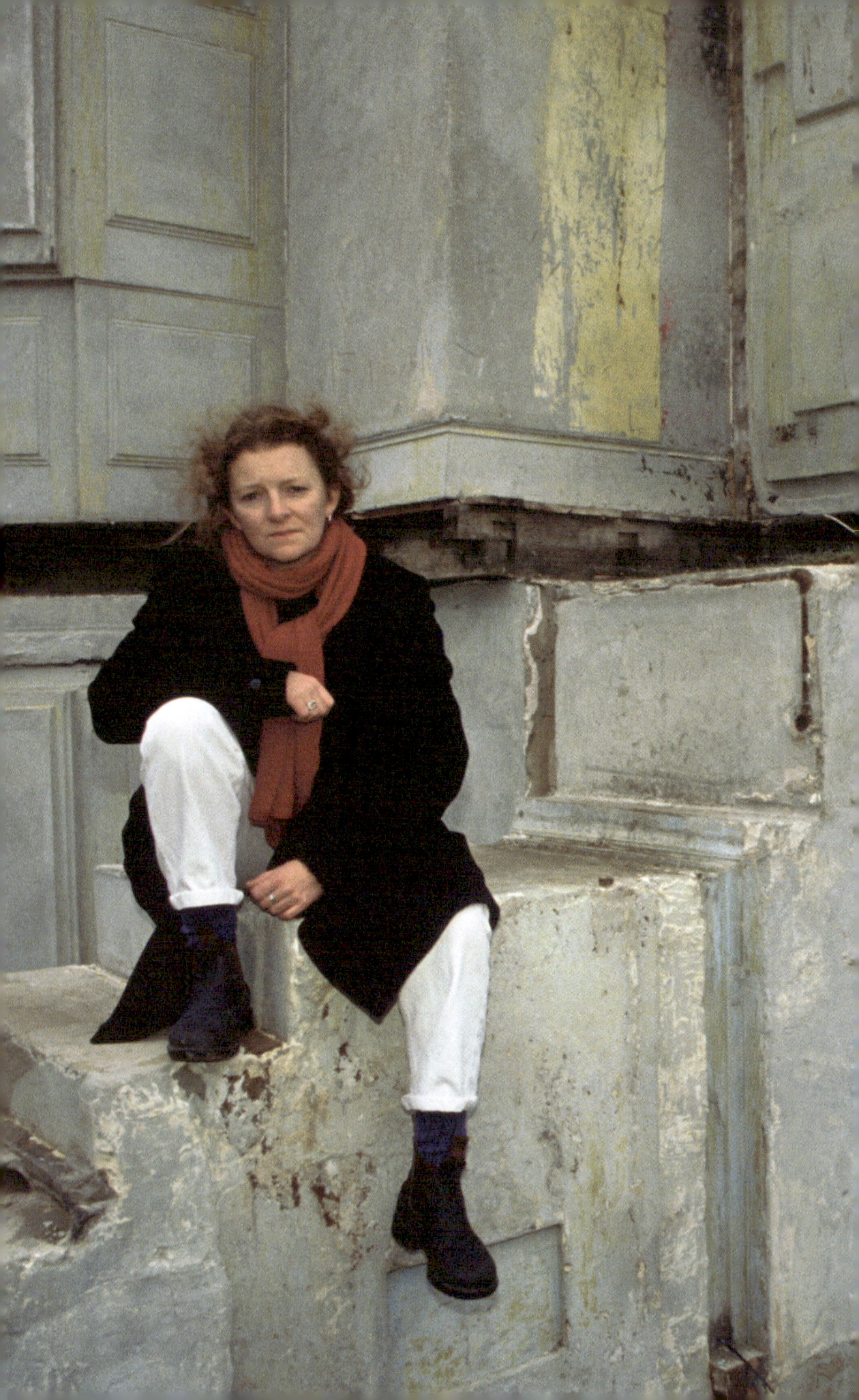

Rachel Whiteread

Rachel Whiteread's *Ghost* was probably the first work that made me see the point of contemporary art. My initial reaction was predictably philistine – what a load of nonsense, just a lump of bare plaster! – but, in time, I found the work haunting and brooded about it for yonks. I went to see her *House* in Mile End in 1993, where she'd cast the last surviving house in a terrace that had been demolished. Some people found it brutal, but I found it unbearably moving. It spoke so poignantly of vanished lives.

Then I read in the papers that it was going to be demolished. There was a press photo of the actual demolition order from Tower Hamlets council, signed by the Leader of the Council. I did a double take when I saw the signature – Eric Flounders. But Eric Flounders was a friend of mine! He had been the press officer for Wings Holidays when I was on the *Sunday Express* in the eighties and had taken me on many riotous press jaunts, including one to Rio de Janeiro where I interviewed the train robber Ronnie Biggs. Later, he switched to Cunard and took me on what was ballyhooed as the first transatlantic crossing of the *QE2* after a major refit. Unfortunately, the refit hadn't been completed when we embarked and there was water sloshing down the corridors. Many of the cabins were unusable, including Eric's. Very kindly, I said he could share mine which meant that for years afterwards he went round telling people that he'd slept with Lynn Barber. (He is gay.)

Anyway, this all meant that I felt Eric owed me a massive favour. I thought that it would be simple: I'd phone him and tell him he mustn't demolish Rachel Whiteread's *House*. So, I rang him and explained my mission and he groaned: 'Oh, not you too.' He said every self-styled art lover in London had been on to him and he was fed up. The only one who made a difference was Doris Saatchi, who persuaded him to extend the demolition deadline by a couple of months. I wrote a short diary item about my failed attempt to become a behind-the-scenes string-puller, which Doris Saatchi must have read as she asked me to lunch. I told her that I was thinking of doing a series of interviews with art collectors. 'Not art collectors!' she exclaimed, 'they're all so boring [she was married to Charles Saatchi]: concentrate on artists, they're the interesting ones.' I took her advice and that's what I did.

I finally got to interview Rachel Whiteread at her studio in the old Yardley soap factory in Carpenters Road in 1996. But God, it was hard work! She *really* didn't like answering personal questions. I learned that her mother, Pat Whiteread, was an artist. Her father was a polytechnic administrator. Both were socialists. The important thing however, she said, was that she was the younger sister of twins – moreover twins who spoke their own private language – and so was born into a two-against-one situation, and always had to fight her corner.

They lived in the Essex countryside till she was seven, then moved to London. She hated school and often hid in her parents' wardrobe – one of the first sculptures she ever made was *Closet*, a cast of a wardrobe. At her comprehensive, she signed up to do science A-levels but at the very last minute switched to art, and found she was 'incredibly thirsty for it'. She discovered casting while she was still at Brighton Polytechnic and carried on doing it when she went to the Slade, where she was lucky to have Phyllida Barlow as her tutor. She made casts of hot-water bottles (she likes them because they look 'like headless, limbless babies') and the spaces under chairs, but then she got on to more ambitious subjects – first *Ghost*, which Charles Saatchi bought, and then *House*, which went on to win the Turner Prize. The K Foundation also awarded it a £40,000 prize for the worst piece of art – she gave the money to Shelter.

In her studio, she showed me two mortuary slabs that were among the first things she ever cast and said, 'I don't really want to talk about my interest in death, but there was a period when I made a lot of work that was obviously connected with it.' She'd been to an architectural salvage yard and bought a ceramic draining board, then asked if they had anything similar but bigger. The man replied: 'Oh, you mean a mortuary slab!' and he had a couple. She bought and cleaned them and 'it was almost like cleaning a body, you know?' One of them still had hairs in the plughole. 'It was just completely revolting, but quite intriguing, too'. Like Damien Hirst, she was fascinated by death and obviously thought about it more than most people her age.

When I saw her, she had just been commissioned to build the Holocaust Memorial in Vienna, which she designed as the cast of an inside-out library. But she hated all the press attention. 'My job is making the work. I don't see myself as having to stand there and justify it or pander to people.' She grumbled a lot more in this vein and complained that she couldn't even go and see *House* when it was being cast because people would ask her for autographs. She had to hide behind a newspaper in her parked car. I found her attitude arrogant and faintly absurd. Why couldn't she give autographs? But of course she is arrogant. When I asked if she considered herself the greatest living British woman sculptor, she said she wasn't sure if Dame

Elisabeth Frink was still alive. I reassured her that she had died in 1993. I got the impression that Rachel would prefer the label without the word 'British' and without the word 'woman', too.

I'm not sure what Rachel made of my article, but she was friendly when I ran into her subsequently and invited me to come and see the disused synagogue she was casting in Chase Street, Bethnal Green. She said she hoped to live there with her husband, the sculptor Marcus Taylor. But they were planning to adopt children, and were unsure whether the adoption authorities would look kindly on sending a child to live in a derelict synagogue in Bethnal Green.

I interviewed her again in 2001 when she was casting *Untitled Monument* for the fourth plinth in Trafalgar Square. It would be the largest resin object ever made, and she was doing it at her own expense, funding it by selling fifteen smaller maquettes so the *Daily Mail* couldn't do its usual screeching about wasting public money. It ran into tremendous difficulties – the first seven maquettes she made with her American plastics team all cracked and she had to postpone the Trafalgar Square opening for six months while they worked out what went wrong. Then, when the American plastics team came back to make the full-sized plinth, they made a very basic miscalculation: they didn't bring enough resin. That was another week's delay, and then it was touch and go whether the cast would be finished on time. It was, just, and looked very beautiful in Trafalgar Square.

In 2018, Artangel, who sponsored *House*, held a dinner to commemorate the twenty-fifth anniversary of the work. It was at a long narrow restaurant in Tower Hamlets, just round the corner from Mile End Park where *House* had stood, so we trooped along to see the

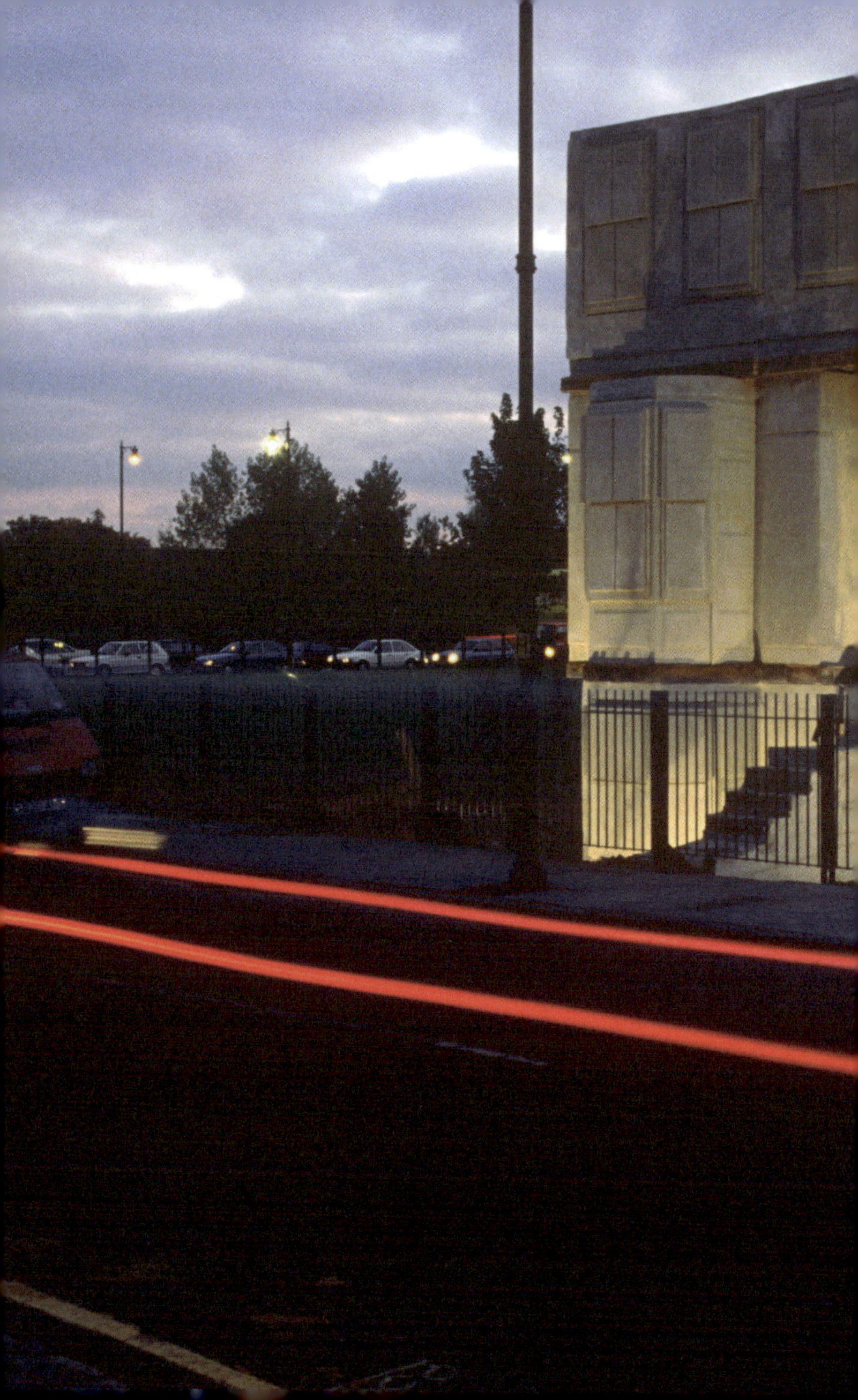

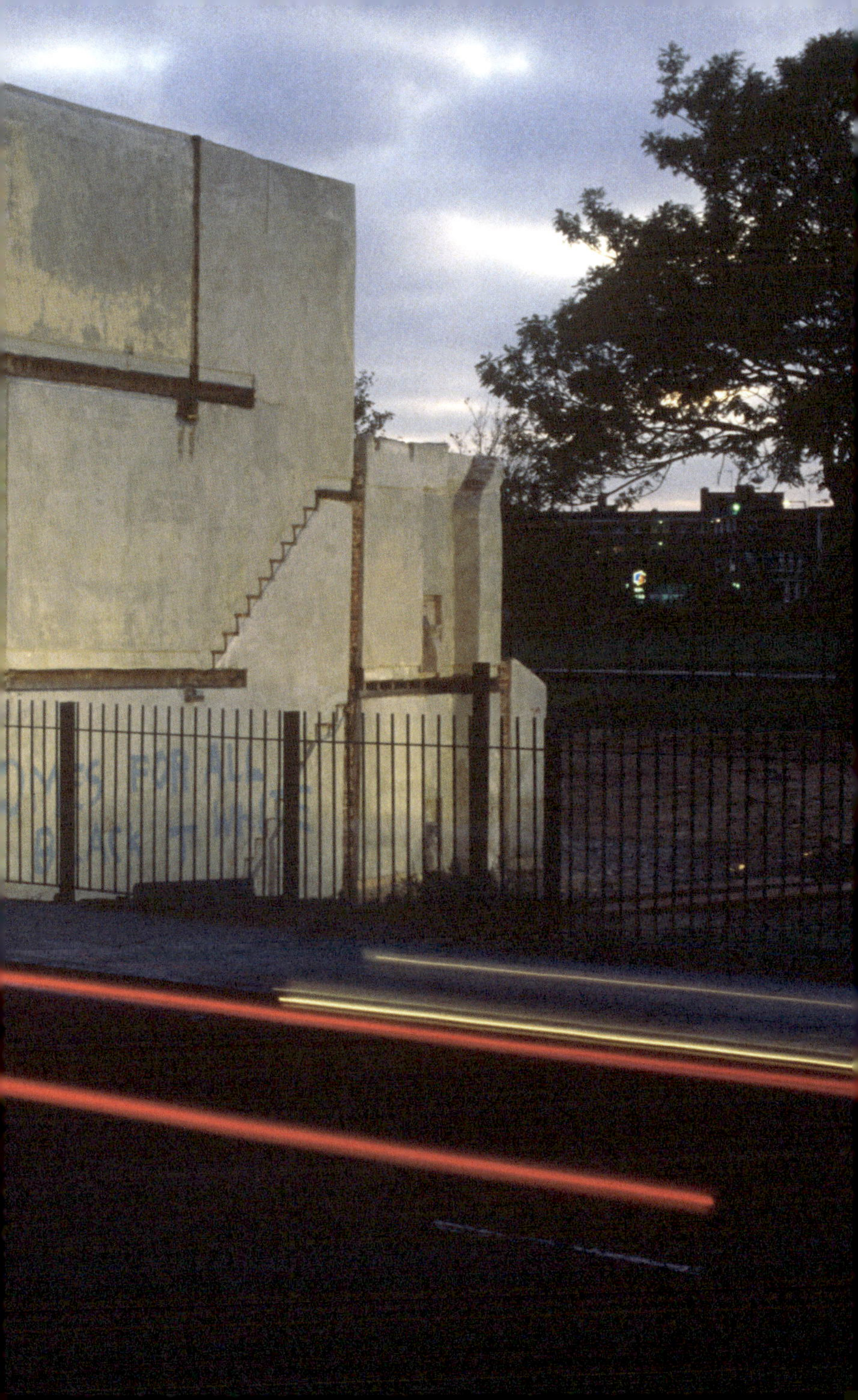

place – now just a dull empty space when it could have been a site of art pilgrimage like Antony Gormley's *Cosby Beach* in Liverpool. I predicted back in 2001 that Rachel Whiteread would be the first of the YBAs to be made a Dame, and she finally was in 2019.

Why did it take so long? And why, why, oh why was *House* ever demolished?

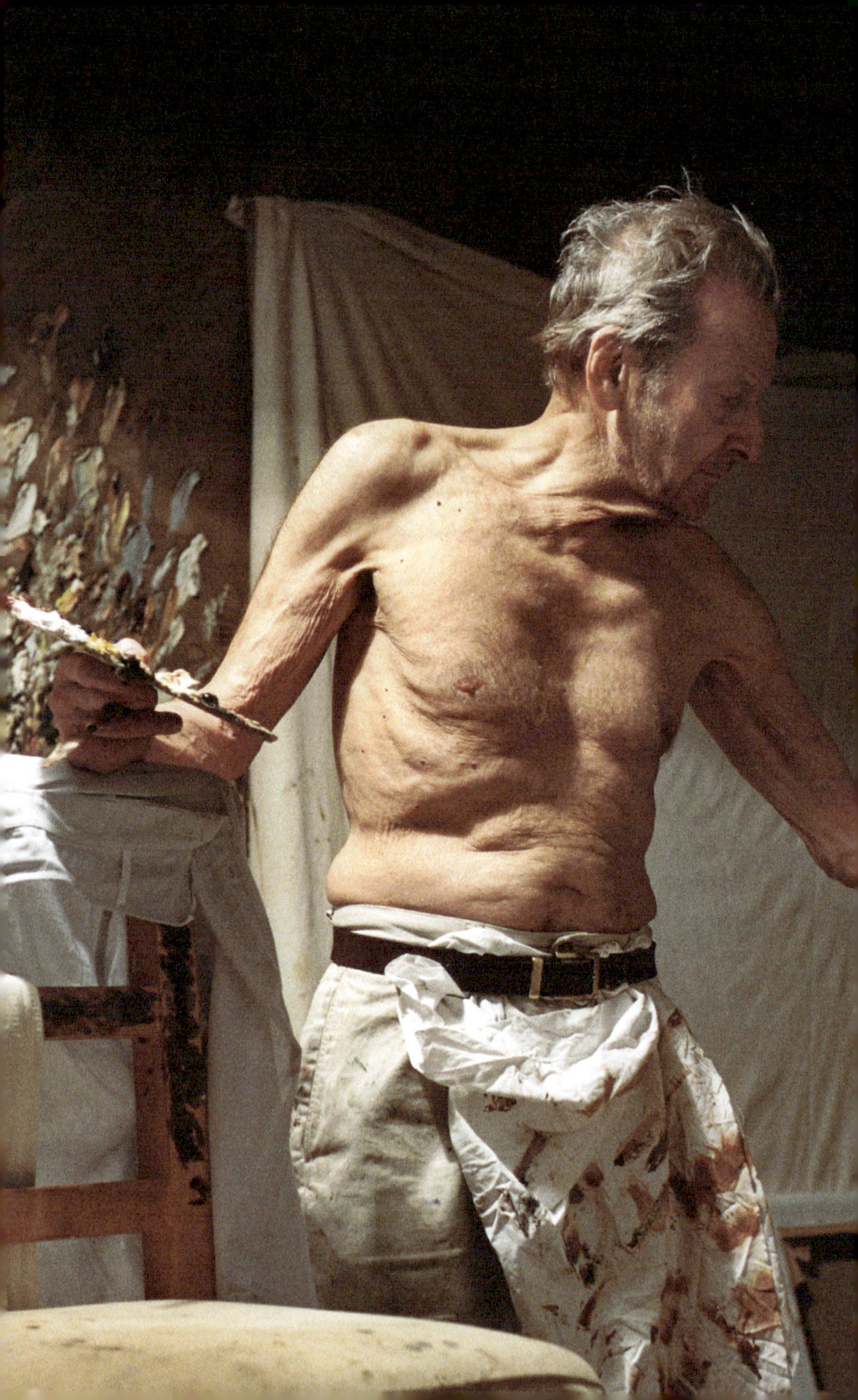

Lucian Freud
The One That Got Away

I spent years trying to get an interview with Lucian Freud – he was always top of my wish list, and I practically stalked him. I wrote to him about once a fortnight and never got a reply. Until one day, I did. I'd said in my letter that I knew he worked almost non-stop but that he must sometimes have to go to the dentist or out for a meal or something and I'd come along as a fly on the wall. This was his reply.

Over the years I got various friends of Freud to appeal on my behalf. The editor Bruce Bernard tried, even Nick Serota promised to put in a plea, but the answer was always no. Then, as I was having lunch one day at Moro in Exmouth Market, I noticed a woman smiling at me across the room. As so often with my hopeless memory, I knew that I knew her but couldn't place her. It was only as she and her companion were leaving that I recognised her: Susannah Chancellor, wife of Alexander Chancellor, and muse of Lucian Freud. And the man she'd been lunching with? Freud himself! And she'd given me such a friendly smile, maybe even inviting me to join them! So, I dashed out of the restaurant – just in time to see them disappearing into a taxi.

In subsequent years, I saw Freud a couple of times at parties and once he said hello, but that was it. After he died, I became friends with the painter David Dawson, who was his studio assistant, sitter, and close friend for many years. Freud left Dawson his Kensington house, so I got to see his studio and bedroom, but that, I'm afraid, is the closest I ever got. At least I have Freud's letter, framed, in the downstairs loo.

10-7-93

Dear Mrs Barber

Your letter to me is based on the assumption that there exists some reason or need for you to interview or write about me. I do, as you rightly suppose, occasionally eat something and (as a result) go to the dentist but that is some way from agreeing to be shat on by a stranger.

Sincerely Lucian Freud

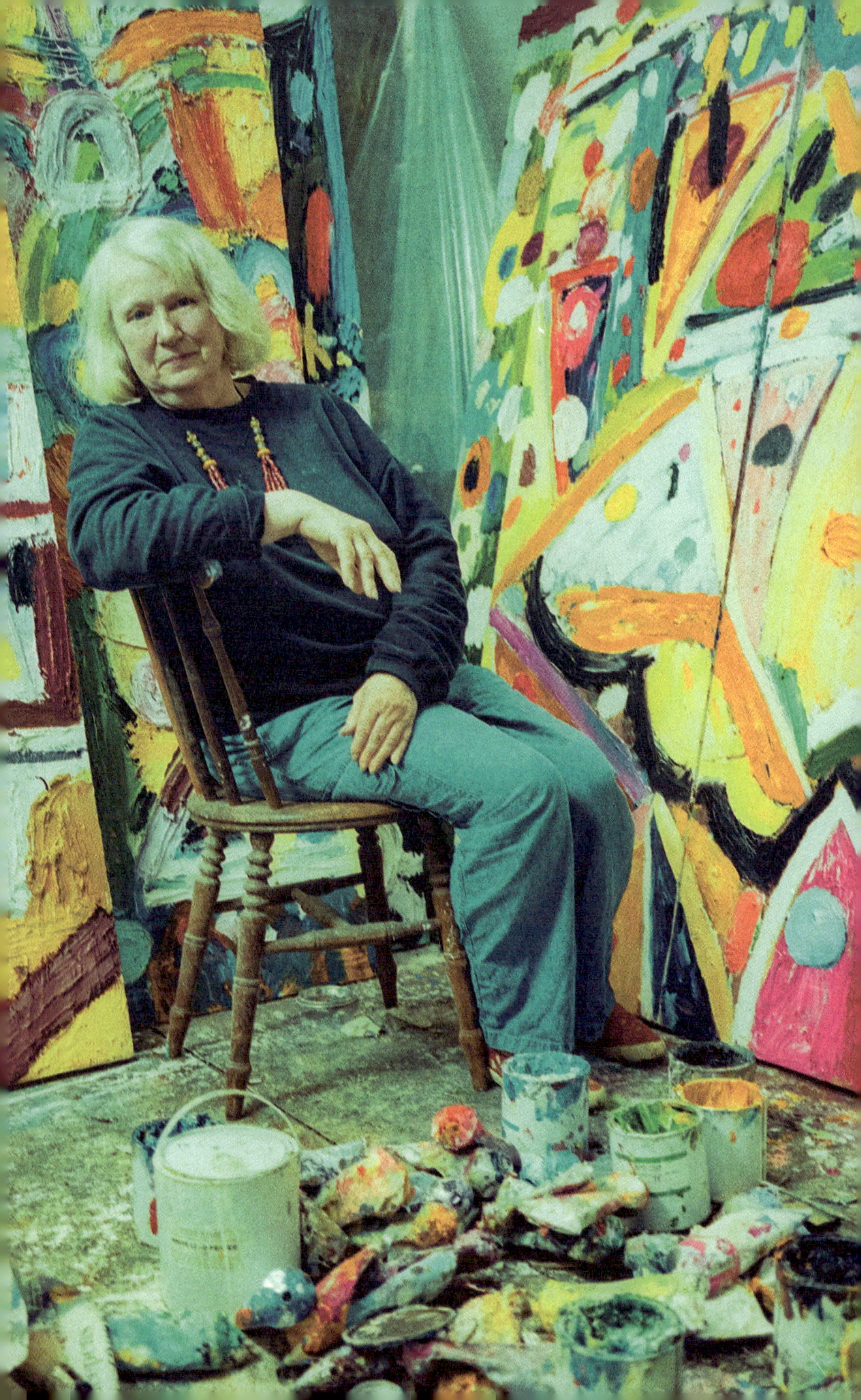

Gillian Ayres

The first time I ever bought any contemporary art was in 1994. David and I quite often bought pictures, but they were always antiques, mainly Victorian watercolours or prints. I used to go to auctions at Phillips where you could pick up sweet little Baxter prints for as little as £3 or £5 – I think the most I ever paid was £10. We also collected Pears Soap prints and 19th century nursery pictures of guardian angels. I remember interviewing the comedian Barry Humphries, who said he used to collect Belgian surrealists before deciding that it was wrong to give money to dealers or auction houses and, instead, that you should only buy from living artists who would get the benefit. I must have registered this idea at the back of my mind because, in 1994, suddenly flush with money having signed a contract with *Vanity Fair*, I decided that for David's birthday, instead of buying another Victorian print, I would buy him a work by a living artist. I remembered that he had a painter friend at Eton, Edmund Fairfax-Lucy, whose work he admired. I made the decision to try to buy a painting of his and was delighted to find a lovely small landscape in the Islington Art Fair.

The painting itself was very expensive, so I thought I'd better take David to see it before I actually bought it. We went round the art fair and I said, 'there's a painting by Edmund Fairfax-Lucy', and David said 'oh yes, it's lovely'. But the paintings he *really* got excited about were two small square abstracts by Gillian Ayres. This was odd because he'd never shown any enthusiasm for abstract art before. They did absolutely zing off the wall, so, later, I went back to the art fair and bought them, I think for £7,500. I remember worrying at the time that, having a lot of pink in them, they would clash with the sitting room's red curtains but when we hung them on the wall, one above the other, they simply dismissed the curtains with a queenly wave.

Over the months, I noticed that one of the paintings was much 'better' than the other though I couldn't pinpoint exactly why. It was just that the top painting was more intriguing, more absorbing. It was always suggesting new possibilities: was it a landscape? Was it a close-up of cheese? Whereas the bottom painting quickly settled into looking like a rainbow over a stream and became increasingly difficult to see any other way. So, when the editor of *Modern Art* asked me to write an article about my first experience of living with abstract art, I addressed this problem and got many interesting responses from readers – several suggesting that I hang the painting upside down, which I tried without much success. But, more importantly, I got a phone call from Gillian Ayres's gallery, Purdy Hicks in those days, saying that Gillian would like to come and visit us and sign the paintings.

Panic! Had we hung them correctly? Had we even hung them the right way up? Should we have had them framed? And would she expect to see other fabulous artworks on our walls? (In which case she was going to be disappointed.) She came anyway, in her paint-spattered clothes, took a brush and paint pot from her capacious handbag, laid a newspaper on the floor, and signed the paintings. She also produced another painting, the same size as the two on our wall, and said this was for when I got bored with the rainbow-over-stream. I thought she meant as a substitute, but no, she was giving it as an extra. So now we were the proud owners of three Gillian Ayreses.

She also said that if we were ever near Morwenstow, on the north Devon coast, where she lived, we must visit her at Tall Trees, which we did the next summer. It was absolutely lovely, driving up

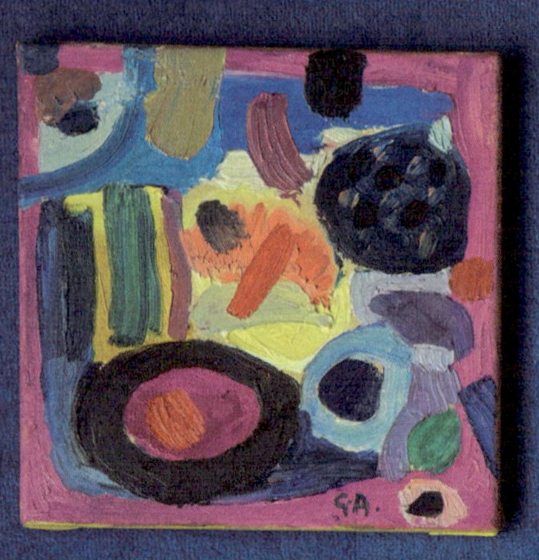

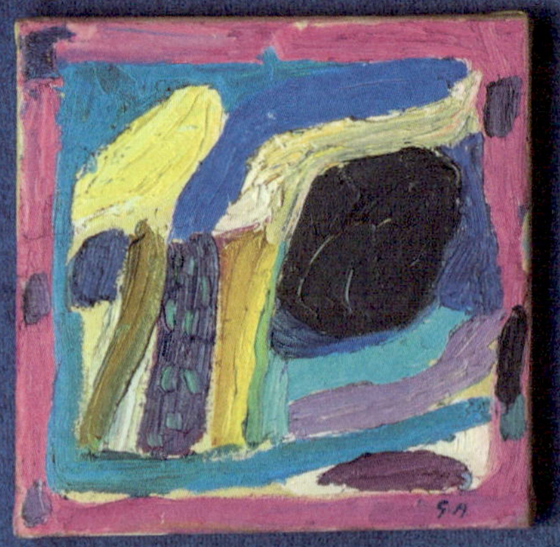

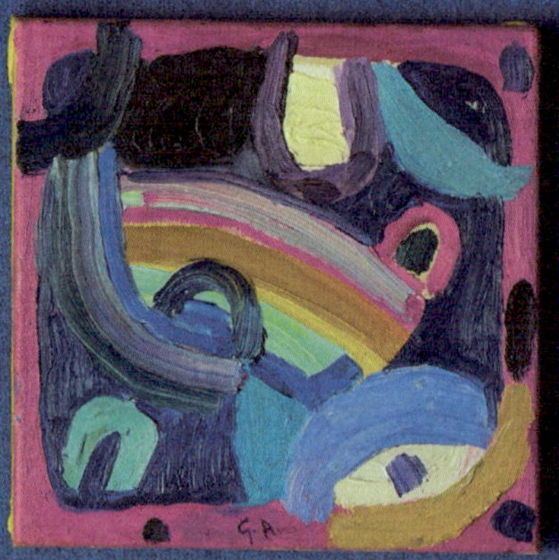

a terrifyingly steep rutted track through near-jungle to her long, low farmhouse on the top of a cliff. She showed us round the house (lovely antiques, walls of art books) and introduced her ex-husband, Henry Mundy. They divorced back in the seventies, but they still lived together. Then she took us into her studio, a huge freezing barn, and showed us her works in progress – wonderful blazing abstracts – and the slit in the wall through which Cadogan Tate handlers would eventually take them away. (It's amazing to think of Cadogan Tate removal lorries driving up that terrifying track but, apparently, they did.)

It was in 1997 that I returned to Tall Trees to interview her for the *Observer*. She was a difficult interviewee, periodically exclaiming 'This is all very *dull*, isn't it?' and 'Terrible women's magazine slush,' But, as always, I was keen to get some basic biography. She grew up in Barnes, in relative affluence – her father ran the family hat-making business – and was educated at St Paul's where her best friend was Shirley Williams, the future founder of the Socialist Democratic Party. She told me that the two of them would claim to be Siamese twins on buses so that they would only pay one fare, and how they broke into an empty house in Cheyne Walk and jumped on the beds. 'I had a sort of wildness then', she told me. 'I wish I had it now.'

She had no artistic background but nevertheless, aged twelve, decided to be a painter. The Slade accepted her at sixteen, with the caveat that she would have to wait two years before enrolling. She went to Camberwell instead but was disappointed. It was all Euston Road influence: 'drab subjects painted with drab accuracy in drab colours.' There were loads of ex-servicemen there, and one of them, eleven years older, was named Henry Mundy, and had fought against the Japanese.

She showed me a photo of her as a stunning young blonde, surrounded by adoring men, including Henry. Was she a sex bomb? 'Absolutely!' Henry told me. 'Everyone fancied her, but they couldn't get anywhere.' Gillian claimed she was not aware of being a sex bomb, but 'Now I look back with slight regret. I wish I'd had a roaring sex life, but I didn't.'

She married Henry, had two sons, Jimmy and Sam, and taught at Corsham, then Winchester until her resignation in 1981. It was a huge financial gamble – it meant selling her London house, and taking Sammy out of Dartington and putting him into a local comp. But she calculated she had enough to live on for three years and then she could work in a supermarket. In fact, the Oxford Museum of Modern Art gave her a show almost immediately and her prices shot up. She divorced Henry and lived with a much younger artist called Gareth Williams on the Lleyn Peninsula in Wales, with peacocks and a pet duck. Henry came to stay for Christmas and stayed on – he and Gareth became good friends. But Gareth was killed on his bike in 1987 and Gillian moved to Devon, followed by Henry.

I told her that what I loved about her work was its exuberant sense of happiness and she said, 'Yes, I want to see that too. I don't like tragedy, really.' And she was not ashamed to say that she aims for beauty. 'People think beauty is sort of slushy or something. I was surprised the other day by Howard Hodgkin saying that he didn't like things to be "*just* beautiful". Why not? I think beauty can lift you up and sort of take your feet away from the ground, but I also think it's very *sensible*.' Quite.

I used to see Gillian a couple of times a year, when she had shows in London and was staying with her son, Sam Mundy, in East

Sheen. She switched to a new gallery, Alan Cristea in Cork Street, and Cristea held wonderful lunches for her where he turned the gallery into a private members' club for the occasion so that Gillian could smoke. She was the most devoted smoker I've ever known; more so than Maggi Hambling, more so, even, than me. In fact, she's the reason I'm still smoking. I once gave up for a few weeks when I tried the miracle pill, Champix, recommended by Stephen Fry. But then I fixed to have lunch with Gillian at the River Cafe in December. There was an absolute white-out blizzard on the day, and I expected her to cancel. When I arrived however, she was already sitting at a table near the entrance and explained, 'I thought we'd sit here, so we can order our food then go out and smoke.' 'Go out?! There's a blizzard out there!' 'Oh, it's all right,' Gillian said, 'the waiters will bring patio heaters.' Which they did. This hardly seemed the moment to break it to Gillian that I'd stopped smoking, so when she lit up, I asked for one. I was a smoker again, standing outside in the snow. I'm grateful to her.

She was very upset by the Momart fire in May 2004 when a whole suite of her Indian paintings from the eighties were destroyed. Her friend Shirley Conran had bought them but, Gillian was upset to learn, had then put them in storage in the vast Momart warehouse in Leyton, east London. In the early hours of 24 May 2004, the warehouse was mysteriously destroyed by a fire that blazed all night. Firefighters could not enter for fear of acetylene cylinders exploding so they let it burn out. It was apparent the following morning that the whole warehouse had gone. An insurance assessor said that they would probably never know whether the blaze was accidental or arson because there was no remaining evidence.

As well as the Ayreses, the fire also consumed fifty major works by Patrick Heron, various Chris Ofilis and Paula Regos, spin paintings by Damien Hirst and also works from his collection including some by Sarah Lucas, Gary Hume and Angus Fairhurst, and the Chapman Brothers' *Hell*. Dinos Chapman remarked, 'If the insurers decide the fire is an act of God it's going to be quite funny – that God destroyed Hell. In fact, if that happens I will start going to church.' But the one I was personally most upset about for reasons I'll explain later was Tracey Emin's tent, *Everyone I Have Ever Slept With, 1963–1995*, though Tracey herself said, 'I just thank God no one was hurt.'

A subsequent fire investigation found that the CCTV camera overlooking the warehouse had been deliberately tampered with and intruders had bored through a brick wall into an industrial unit packed with consumer electronics. There were thirty-four such units on either side of the Momart warehouse and the burglars probably had no idea that there was a great art store inside. Nor indeed did the fire brigade. Passers-by began noticing flames coming out of the building and called the fire brigade at 3.43 a.m. Three fire engines were dispatched to deal with 'a fire in a factory', but by the time they got there, they found an inferno raging. Eventually, fifteen fire engines in total were dispatched. It was obvious by the time they arrived that the building could not be saved however, and the senior fire officer ordered all his men to retreat. Still, no one knew that it contained a priceless store of twentieth-century art. It was only much later that day that Momart started contacting owners. Shirley Conran had to break the news to Gillian Ayres that her paintings had been lost.

Gillian carried on painting (and smoking) well into her eighties, but finally died in 2018 aged eighty-eight. (Henry Mundy outlived her and was a hundred when he died in 2019.) I felt she never really got her due – she should have been made a Dame and I know that Andrew Marr and others campaigned on her behalf – but she was a difficult customer, who often had rows with her galleries and with the Royal Academy. I miss her still, but at least I have her lovely paintings to remind me of her.

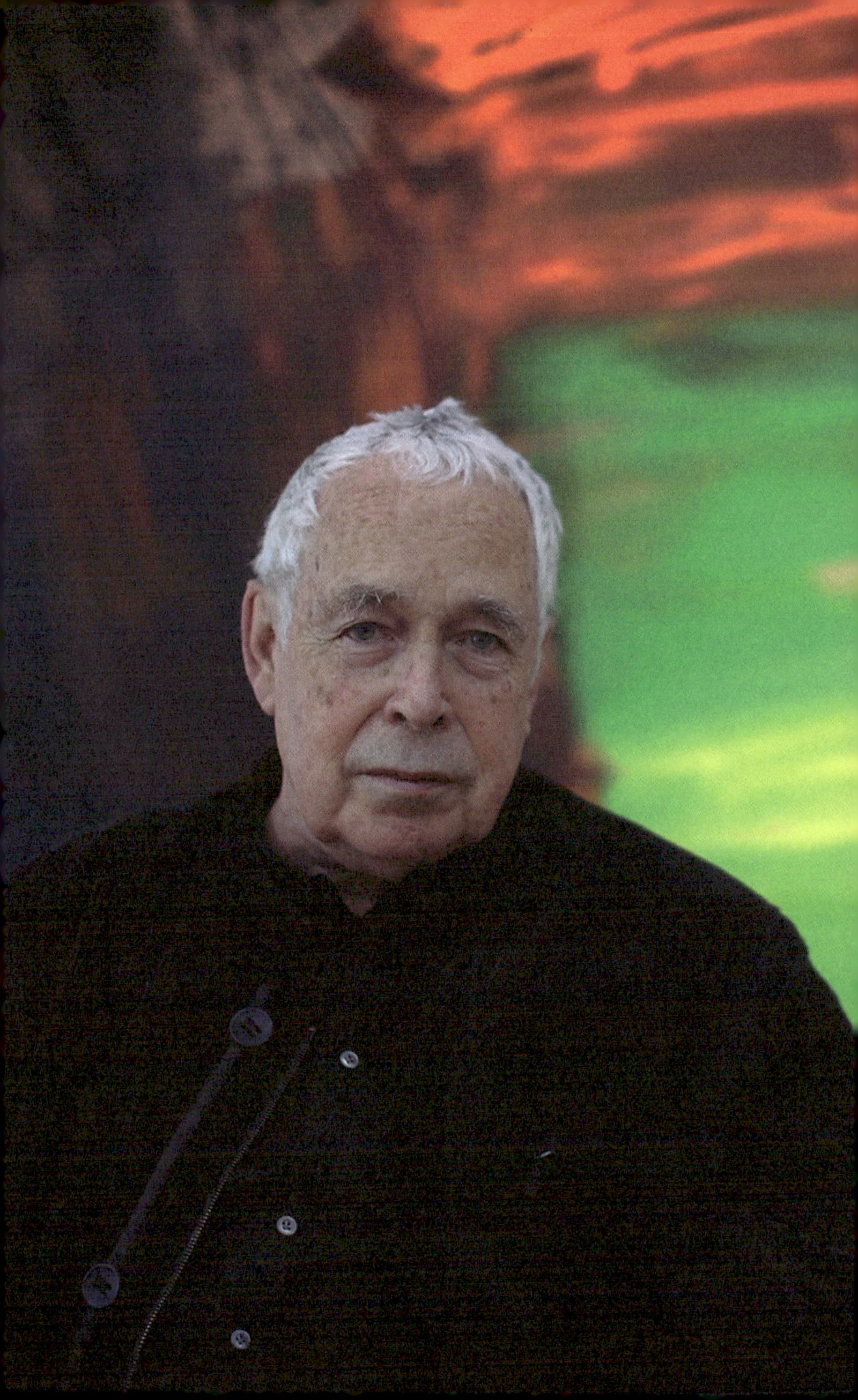

Howard Hodgkin

Howard Hodgkin was so nervous about being interviewed by me that he insisted on lots of preliminary lunches, so he could find out what I was going to ask him. I always think these talks about talks are a waste of time. (My worst was when Theresa May invited me to tea at the House of Commons so she could decide whether she wanted to be interviewed – she didn't, it turned out.) Having lunch with Howard Hodgkin was no hardship however because he took me to such good restaurants and always insisted on paying. He also arranged for me to have a 'private viewing' of his new work at the Anthony d'Offay gallery. I'd never done this before, or since, but it's routine for collectors or potential buyers, apparently – you're shown into a very nice separate gallery with a painting on the wall and a comfortable armchair. The handsome assistant asks what you'd like to drink, then leaves you for as long as you want and tells you to ring the bell when you'd like to see a different painting. It made me insanely self-conscious. I kept wondering if there was a spy camera somewhere and how long I'd got to sit looking before I could ring the bell. Frankly, I wished I'd brought a book.

All the lunches with Hodgkin were good fun though, and it was lucky he was well known at the posh restaurants he took me to because his paint-stained hands and scruffy clothes would have put most waiters off. Also, his habit of bursting into tears. Friends had warned me about this, but still it was disconcerting to see a 67-year-old man, with shaking shoulders, blubbing into his table napkin. The worst was when I said I loved his paintings (which I do) but hated their titles – *A Henry Moore at the Bottom of the Garden, Dinner in Palazzo Albrizzi, On the Riviera, After Visiting David Hockney.* I could understand, I told him, that he didn't want to call his paintings *Symphony in Green* or *Black*, but couldn't he just title them with a date, to get away from these deadly posh jet-setter associations? Waldemar Januszczak, the art historian, made the same point when he said Hodgkin's art seemed to be 'devoted to various ways of getting away from Britain in December'. Hodgkin gave a little yelp and burst into tears. 'Of all the horrible things to say, that's outrageous. My titles are the pictures, and the pictures are the titles. I'm not just hurt; I'm absolutely appalled by what you say ... You have cut me in half.' I thought I'd blown it, but in fact the next week he invited me round to his studio to see one of his new paintings and he was fine. And I do seriously love his paintings – I just hated him crying.

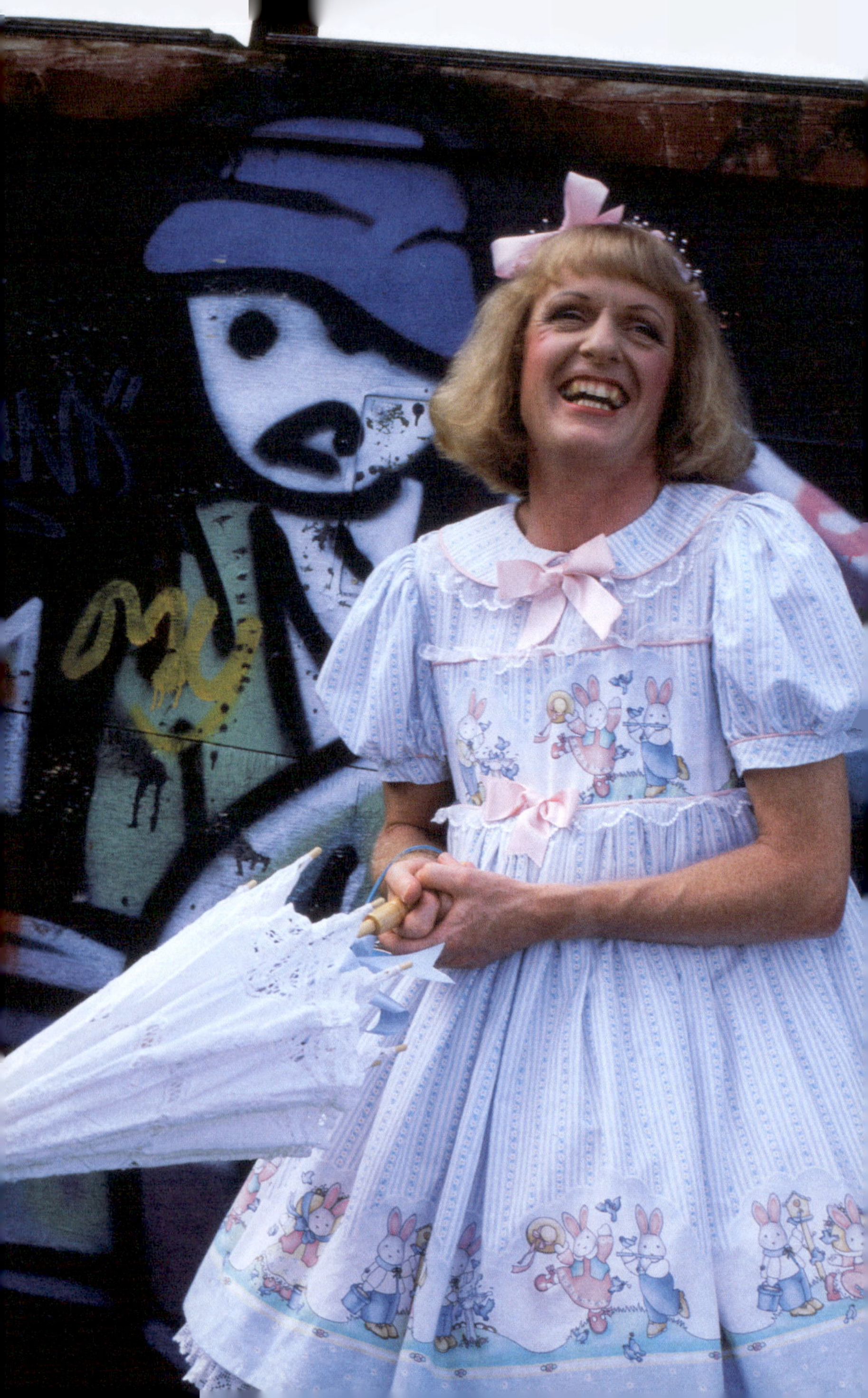

Grayson Perry

Many people, including me, had never heard of Grayson Perry till he won the Turner Prize in 2003 (and there were rumours at the time that he only won because the Chapman Brothers, who were expected to win, put on such a disappointing show). But boy! What a great addition to the pantheon of British art he proved to be – not only as an artist but as a brilliant curator (vide his British Museum show, *The Tomb of the Unknown Craftsman*) and then as an incomparable TV communicator in his Channel 4 documentaries about issues of taste and class. He also wrote a fascinating autobiography, *Portrait of the Artist as a Young Girl*, about growing up as a transvestite, which of course is what first piqued my interest.

When I worked for *Penthouse*, I interviewed quite a few cross-dressers, but I could never understand what transvestism was *about*. Unlike the drag queens I'd met, the transvestites I knew always seemed to focus on the most boring aspects of being a woman – one man droned on about how he liked to get dressed in his pinny and Marigolds and really tackle the limescale round the sink. But Grayson, dressed as say Little Bo Peep in his guise as Claire, seemed the opposite of that. He certainly wasn't pretending to be a housewife; he was more like a little girl dressed in her best party dress.

He explains in his autobiography that his transvestism grew out of fear of his stepfather, an amateur wrestler with a nasty temper. Grayson spent much of his childhood in his bedroom developing his rich fantasy world, which somehow involved dressing up. As a teenager, he would get changed in the public loos in Chelmsford cemetery and traipse around the gravestones in a frock. Despite the chaos at home, he managed to pass nine O-levels and two A-levels but when he left for art school (Portsmouth Poly) his stepfather told him, 'Don't came back.' He dropped all contact with his mother when she told his wife Philippa, 'You must be desperate to marry a transvestite.' He did not attend her funeral in 2016.

Philippa has never minded him being a transvestite – in fact, for their first date, he gave her the choice of going to a club for transvestites, or to a private view. She chose the club. When she went to pick him up, she didn't recognise the woman who came to the door – she thought Grayson must be living with his mother. But anyway, they got on fine and married in 1992. How, I remember asking him, did he explain to their daughter, Flo, that Daddy sometimes wore a frock? 'I've never had to. I never feel I need to justify myself.' There is a photo in his autobiography of Flo, aged five, with Daddy in a frock. And not a glamorous Claire frock but a frumpy housewife frock.

He says he doesn't dress up as much as he used to, maybe just once a week, though of course he dresses as Claire for parties because 'people expect it'. And nowadays Central Saint Martin's art school has a competition for students to design new outfits for Claire, so he is obliged to show them off. But he feels it's not so exciting because it's not scary any more. 'If I wander into the street in a dress now, it's like, oh, there's Grayson Perry – which is not the reaction I want ... It's boring. Nobody notices.' Could he ever give it up? 'What, being a tranny? Oh no, your sexuality is hard-wired.'

I remember once bumping into him, in full Claire mode, at a *Guardian* summer party and introducing him to Tony Benn. 'Grayson is a potter, Mr Benn,' I explained. 'Ah yesh,' said Tony Benn, and started talking seamlessly about the 1842 Stoke-on-Trent pottery riots

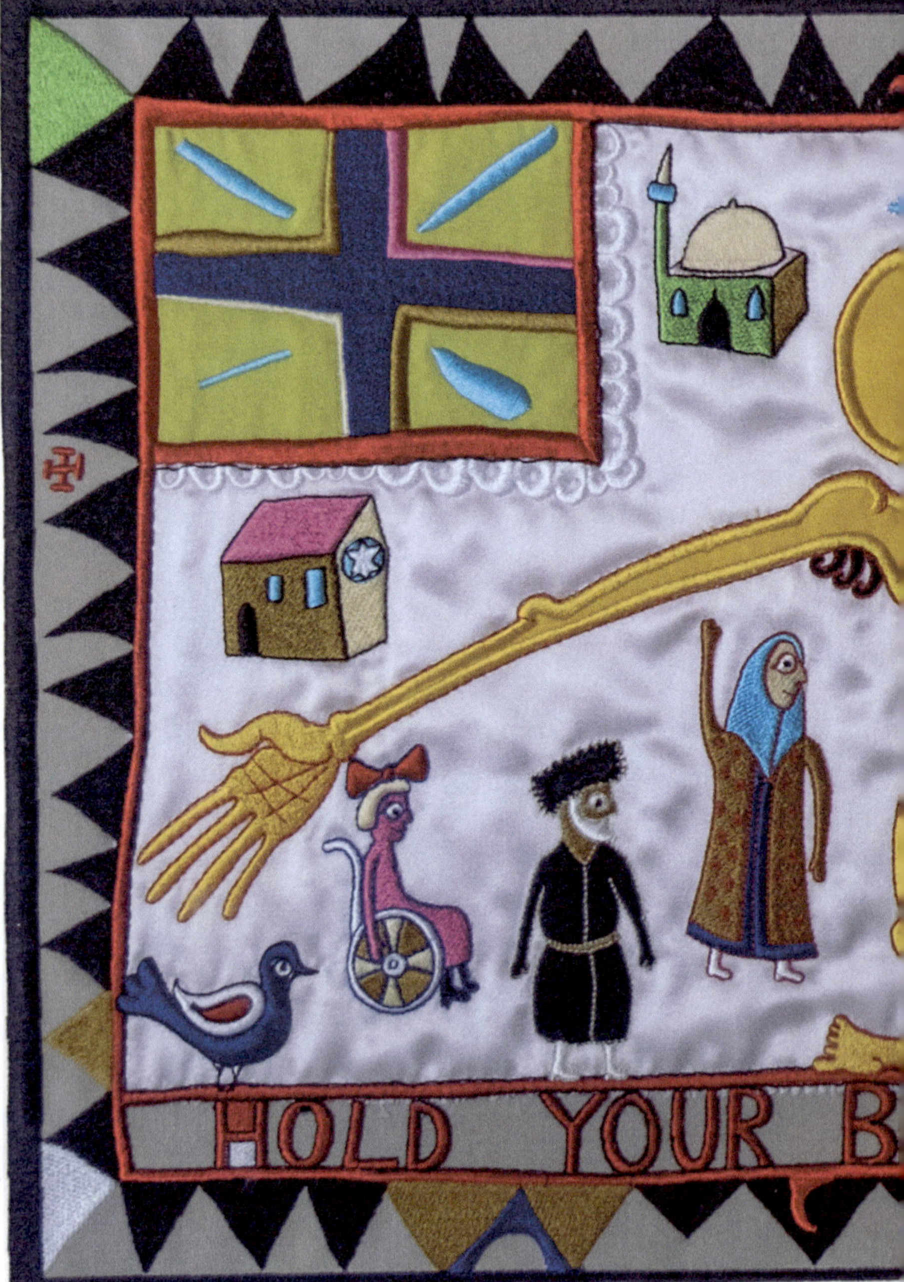
HOLD YOUR B

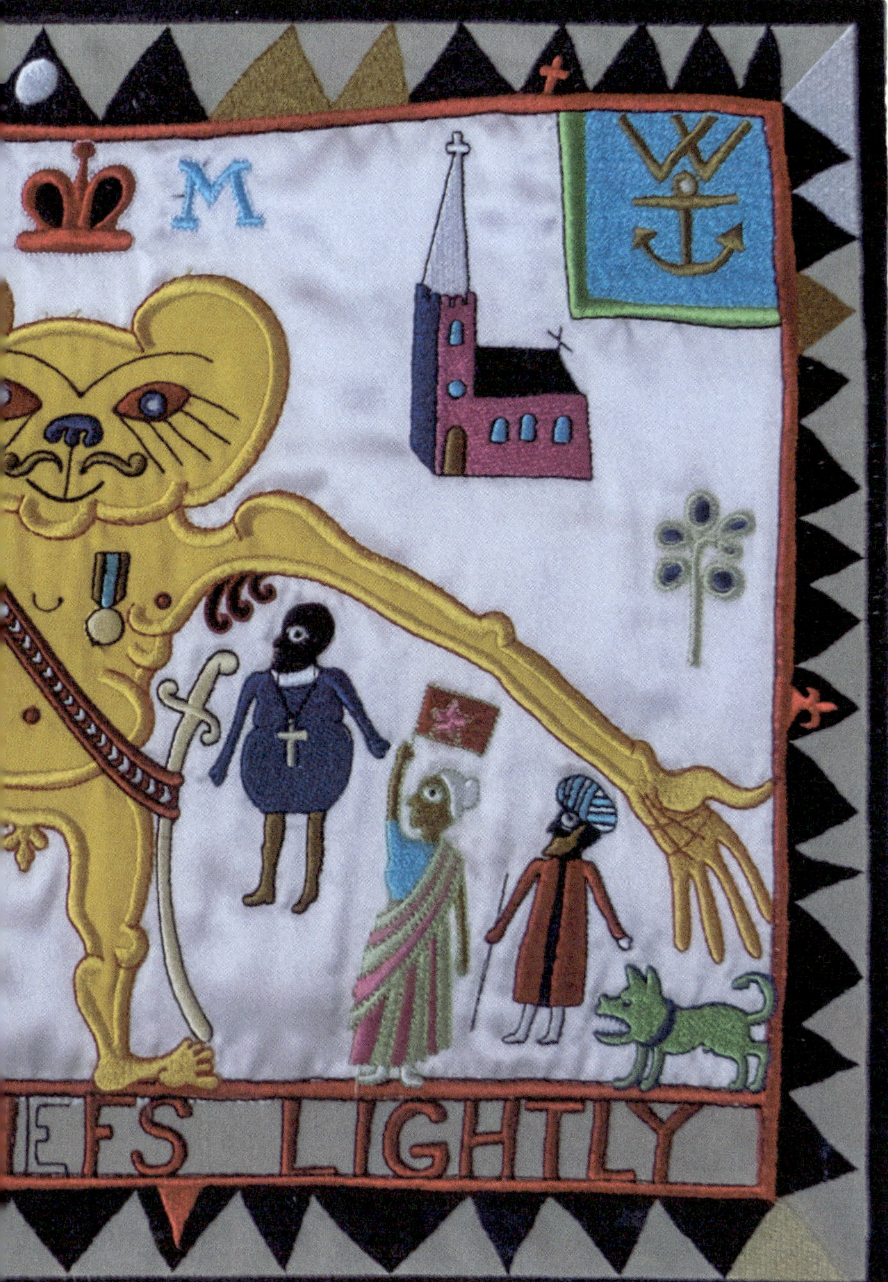
M
IEFS LIGHTLY

and the part they played in the birth of the trade union movement. I wanted to scream 'Does Grayson *look* like a horny-handed son of toil?' Grayson, as always, listened politely. I don't think Benn even noticed that he was wearing a dress.

In 2012, Grayson started making tapestries. He said he'd had a long break from potting when he did his British Museum show, and when he went back to it, he kept thinking, 'Christ, it's so slow!' So now he preferred making tapestries because he could design them in Photoshop and send them off to a factory in Flanders that would manufacture them for £10,000 a pop. Six tapestries were enough for a show, whereas he had to make at least twenty pots to fill a gallery. He did make one new pot that year which he called *Picasso Napkin Syndrome*, since Picasso could pay his restaurant bills simply by signing a napkin. Grayson wasn't yet in that league, but he was aware now that when he made a drawing, he was actually printing money. For a while it made him constipated about drawing but then he resolved to only draw in sketchbooks, which he knew he would never sell, and not on loose sheets of paper. He likes to draw while drinking beer and watching crap television, because that way he feels less self-conscious.

Grayson's Art Club, produced during the lockdown, showed his real genius for inspiring people – even people who didn't think they had any interest in art. It was fitting that he was knighted in the King's first New Year Honours in 2023.

Grayson Perry has probably done more to popularise art in this country than any other artist, with the possible exception of Hockney. I have no idea whether he has also popularised transvestism.

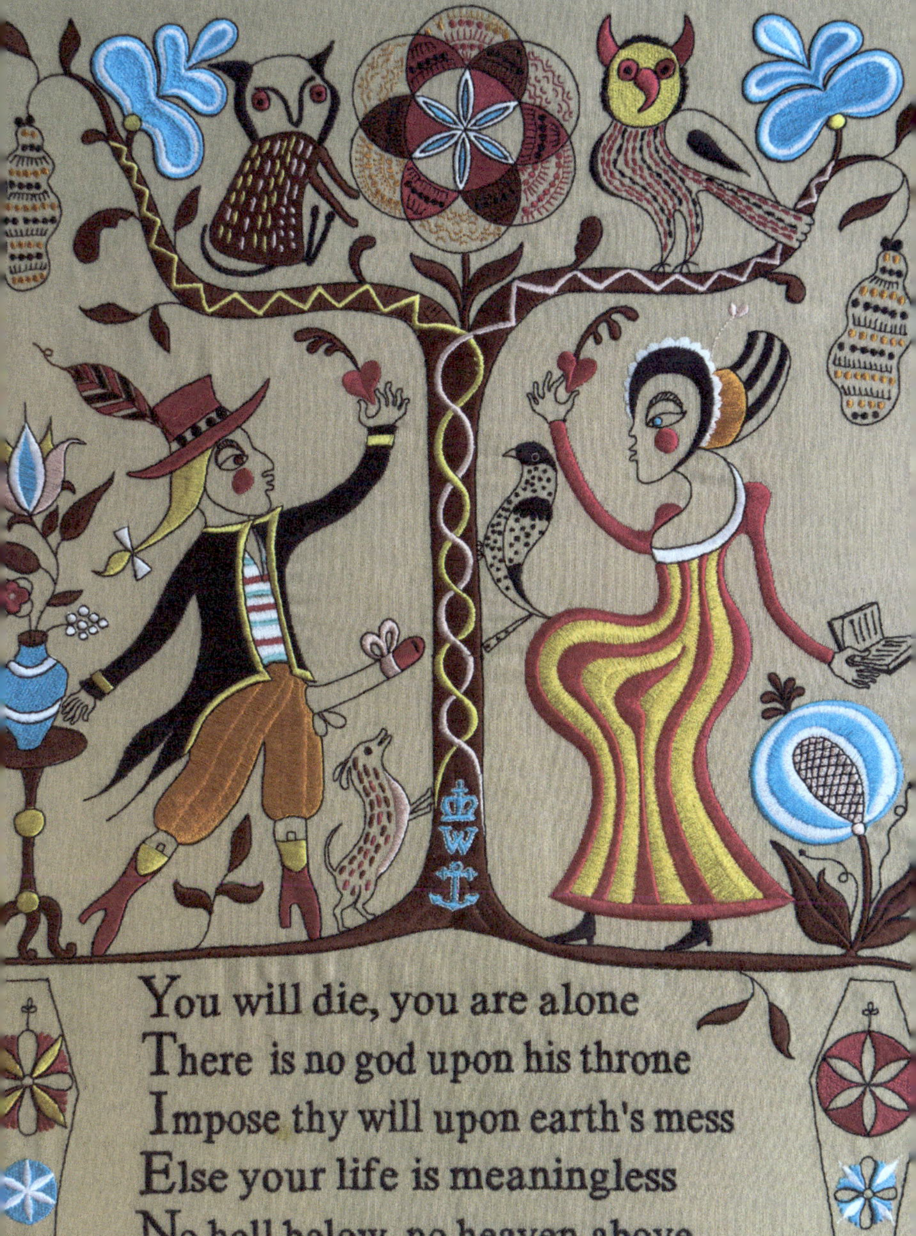

You will die, you are alone
There is no god upon his throne
Impose thy will upon earth's mess
Else your life is meaningless
No hell below, no heaven above
Live life now and act with love .

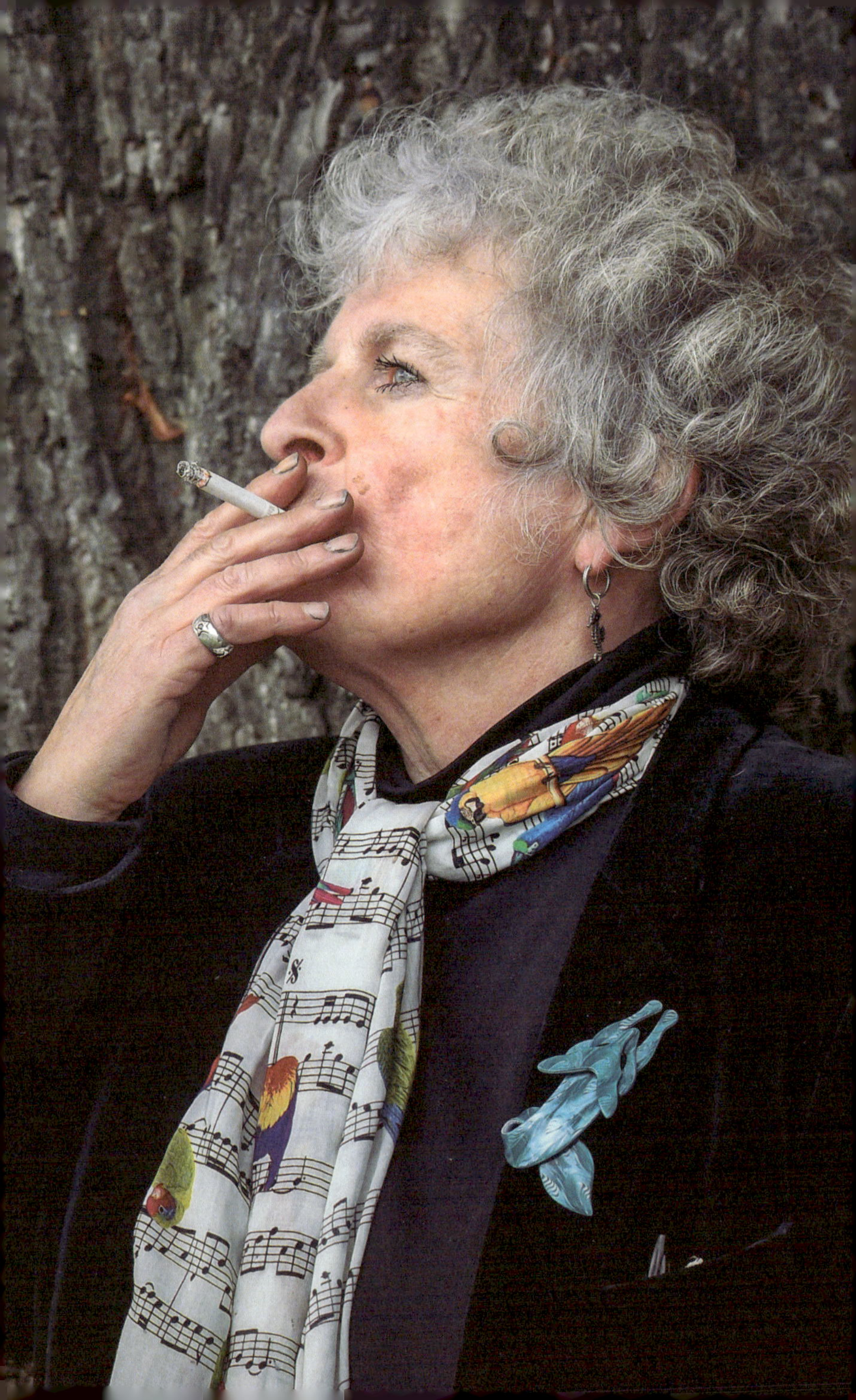

Maggi Hambling

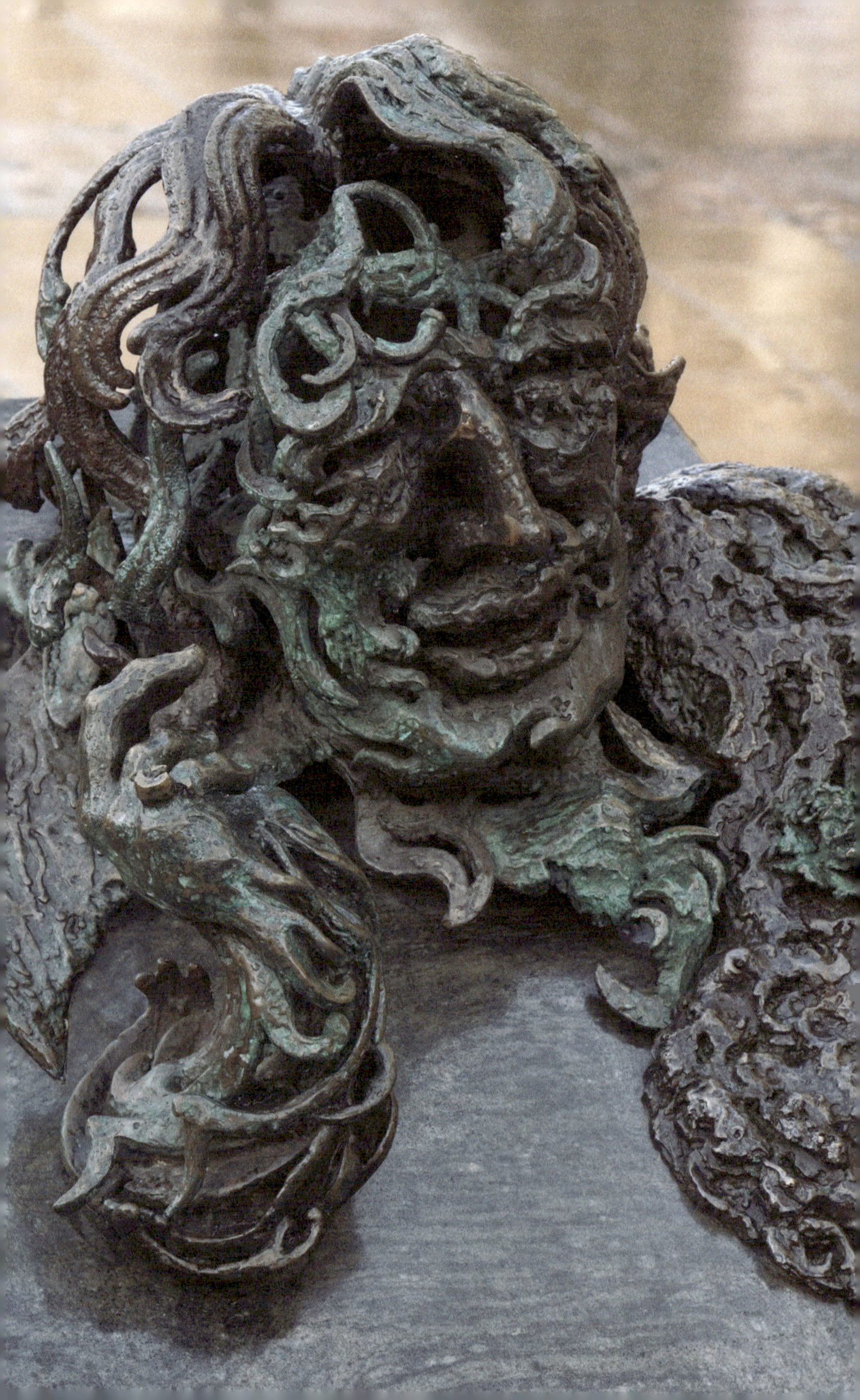

I blow hot and cold about Maggi Hambling. I think her drawings of Henrietta Moraes dying are among the greatest artworks of the twentieth century, but I also think that her sculpture of Oscar Wilde in his coffin in Charing Cross is one of the most hideous. God knows there are plenty of hideous public sculptures in London. When I saw the pictures of Black Lives Matter protesters demolishing the statue of Edward Colston in Bristol, I thought what a good idea – quite apart from Colston's connection with slavery, it was a crap sculpture that fully deserved to die. At the time, there seemed to be a movement in favour of killing statues so then I thought of all the statues in London that should be executed. Maggi Hambling's Oscar Wilde, and now her Mary Wollstonecraft at Newington Green; the monstrous *Kiss* at St Pancras Station, Princess Diana and two random children in the gardens of Kensington Palace, the baffling horse's head outside the Dorchester in Park Lane, the ghastly statue of Churchill and Roosevelt chatting on a bench in New Bond Street – demolish the lot. Actually, it would be easier to draw up a list of London sculptures I would fight to *save* – the Albert Memorial, the Queen Victoria Memorial in front of Buckingham Palace, Charles Sargeant Jagger's statue of the unknown soldier on platform 1 of Paddington Station and his bronze statue of Ernest Shackleton on the side of the Royal Geographical Society in Exhibition Road, and Martin Jennings' statue of John Betjeman at St Pancras. If/when someone is commissioned to do a statue of the late Queen Elizabeth, I hope it's Martin Jennings.

I first interviewed Maggi Hambling at her studio in Clapham. The room was dominated by a hideous Triffid plant called Esmeralda, and it was a relief to go up to see her at her home in Suffolk in 2014, where she spends most of her time. She was preparing an exhibition of her sea paintings, *Walls of Water*, for the National Gallery, and was very excited to be going back to the National Gallery where she was their first-ever artist in residence in 1980. She had a studio upstairs with billboards outside which read 'Meet a Real Artist' and members of the public would wander in and ask daffy questions like 'Do you see auras?' The great thing was that she was allowed to wander round the gallery out of hours and really get to know all the paintings.

She took me to see the suite of new sea paintings housed in a temperature-controlled barn, which had been built on rollers so that it counted as a temporary structure for planning permission. They were knockout but she told me off for asking questions: 'I do think it's very important to approach a painting in silence. Looking at paintings is more difficult than watching TV.' She was happy when I said the paintings seemed to get wilder as they went on, almost like Jackson Pollock. 'Yes, I admire Pollock, I admire his risk-taking. It's all about being *alive* and bringing everything into that one moment.'

After the barn, she took me to her painting studio which has the words 'Stiffen the sinews, summon up the blood' on the door and a litter of cigarette stubs underfoot. She was meant to have given up smoking when she turned fifty-nine, as her father did, and she managed to do so for four years, but had found herself watching a JCB lifting an enormous bronze wave sculpture: 'It was absolutely nerve-wracking. *And* it was my birthday. So, I said, fuck it, anyone got a fag? And went on to smoke the whole packet. I must say, smoking is so much better the second time around.'

Then she took me to the main house where her partner, Tory

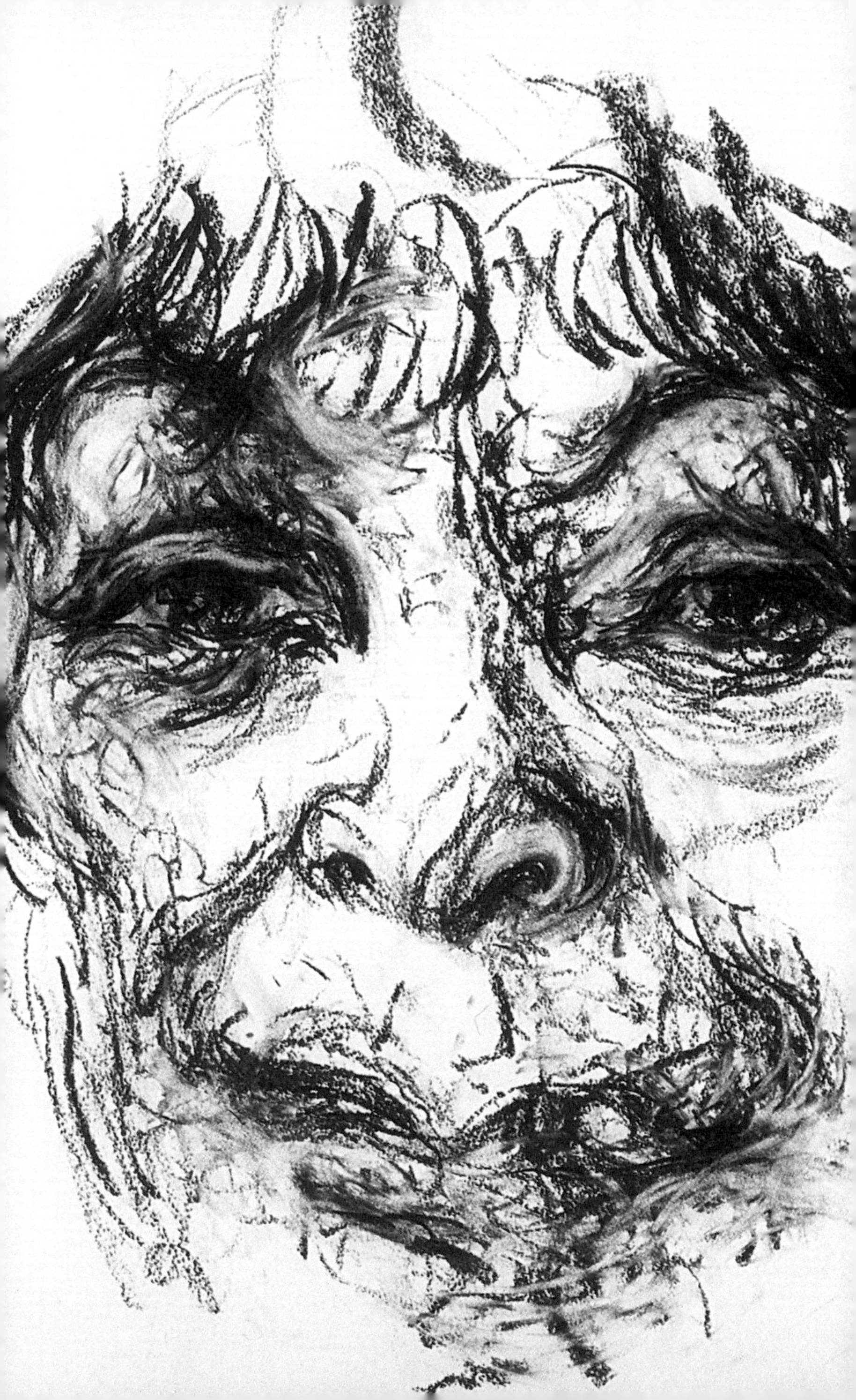

Lawrence, former wife of Lord Oaksey, was preparing lunch (Maggi doesn't cook). They have been together over thirty years, but when I asked Maggi if she thought of it as a marriage, she said, 'It's a *war*! We argue about practically everything.' Over lunch, Maggi told Tory off for eating cream (bad for her arthritis) and Tory told Maggi off for smoking. Maggi complained that their new neighbours in London kept asking them to dinner, but 'They don't have an ashtray! They made me smoke in the garden! There's too much fucking health everywhere!'

She is now seventy-seven, still smoking, still painting, and still giving art classes in London. 'You've got to keep that sort of independent spirit, and keep it alive,' she says. 'I feel younger and freer

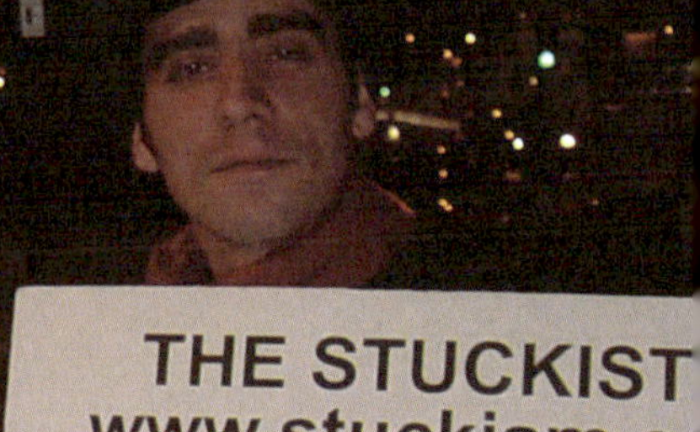
STUCKISTS
stuckism.com
s wrong of
e Tate to
ggest that
he public's
iews will be
taken into
account"
Lynn Barber
Turner Prize judge

THE STUCKIST
www.stuckism.co
"IS IT
ALL A
FIX?
Lynn Barbe
Turner Prize judg

Turner Prize Judge

now than I ever have before.'

On 15 April 2005, I received an invitation from Stephen Deuchar, then director of Tate Britain, asking me to serve as a juror for the 2006 Turner Prize. I was so amazed I had to read the letter several times before I believed it, and then ran around showing it to everyone I knew – even the rather baffled window cleaner who happened to come that day. Most of my friends laughed their heads off but none of them actually said not to do it. Even Tracey, after she'd laughed *her* head off said, 'Yeah, do it. But don't nominate me.' She was still bruised from not having won for *My Bed*.

I never found out why I was chosen, though someone subsequently explained that they always tried to have an outsider, someone who was not professionally involved in the art world, as a contrast to the other three jurists. It was quite hard to find outsiders who went to lots of contemporary art shows.

About a month after I received the letter, Deuchar invited me and my fellow jurors to a meeting at Tate Britain. One, Matthew Higgs, who ran the White Columns gallery in New York, couldn't come because of visa problems, but I met the other two: Andrew Renton, who taught curating at Goldsmiths, and Margot Heller, who ran the South London Gallery. Deuchar explained that our job was to go around shows for a year and choose the artists we wanted to nominate, then meet again in May 2006 to hammer out a shortlist of four. The chosen artists would then have a few months to prepare their individual shows for the Tate, and we would finally meet again in December 2006 to choose the winner.

I went to see the gallerist Sadie Coles the following day, who duly laughed her head off, then said: 'You'll need this.' She handed me a newsletter listing all the current contemporary art shows in Great Britain and Ireland. There were 198 in London alone! I had no idea. Moreover, many of them were in parts of London – east of Hackney, south of Peckham – I had never penetrated. That first weekend, I thought I'd 'do' the Bethnal Green-Shoreditch area, which has the highest concentration of galleries in Britain, but I only managed to see about a dozen. Many of them were shut; a lot were simply unfindable, even with a map; often the video/DVD/sound installation was awaiting repair. The only high point was seeing the actor Keanu Reeves in a Vyner Street gallery admiring an artwork that looked like a blue Formica offcut. I overheard him describing it as 'almost Kleinian' – which is artspeak for blue – and the gallerist telling him it cost twenty grand. I don't know if he bought it.

At first my friends were keen to accompany me on my art expeditions, but they soon dropped off – it was depressing to drive for miles and then find yourself in, say, Balham looking at an installation consisting of three slabs of concrete and a tyre. I should have asked Sadie to mark my card, to tell me which shows were worth seeing, but I was keen to think of myself as a fresh eye, untainted by art-world opinions. What a clot.

The effect of looking at an awful lot of art in a short space of time, and with an increasingly bad temper, as I did, is that your judgement goes haywire. So much passes in a blur that if you find anything at all different or memorable, you are prepared to hail it as the next Picasso. I remember coming home from the Baltic in Newcastle and telling my daughter, Rosie: 'I saw some exciting sculpture made of carpet fluff!'

She stared at me. 'What was exciting about it?' 'Well, it was a room with a fitted carpet,' I blathered, 'and the artist had scraped some of the carpet fluff into little piles to look like things.' 'So could you hoover it up?' Rosie asked. Some people are such philistines.

The consolation for all these unfruitful expeditions was the limitless number of art parties I was invited to. Once word spread that I was a Turner Prize juror, gallerists and collectors clamoured to meet me – one even offered to fly me to Basel on his private plane. And I was invited to more and more art dinners which are where the VIPs go while the liggers are finishing off the free beer and vodka at the preview. I liked the parties but soon got bored with the dinners. They were always held in very posh restaurants, but the guests were rarely artists: instead they were collectors, curators, museum directors, gallerists and those mysterious 'art consultants' who tell people like Leonardo DiCaprio what to buy. I never knew who anyone was and was always putting my foot in it: I asked some Italian bloke if he ran a gallery, and he said yes. 'Oh, what's it called?' 'The Uffizi.'

In December, halfway through my jurorship, I was invited to the dinner for the 2005 Turner Prize-giving. It was an oddly tense evening, because the Tate was under attack for buying Chris Ofili's *The Upper Room* – thirteen paintings of rhesus macaque monkeys resting on lumps of elephant dung – and Nick Serota made an impassioned speech defending it, which rather overshadowed the actual prize-giving. I'd been confidently telling all my friends that Jim Lambie was bound to win and even advised my editor to put a bet in it, so I almost fainted when the winner was announced as Simon Starling for his *Shedboatshed* in which he had dismantled a shed, turned it into a boat, paddled it down the Rhine, and then rebuilt it as a shed.

That night I wailed to my diary, 'For the first time, I find myself seriously wondering – is it all a fix? After six months as a Turner Prize juror, I feel as adrift as on the day I started, thoroughly demoralised, disillusioned, and full of dark fears that I have been stitched up – that the art world (whatever that is) has already decided who will win the 2006 Turner Prize and that I am brought in purely as a fig leaf.'

It didn't help that we jurors were supposed to have been sent a list of all the eligible shows we should be going to which I hadn't received, and was worried that many of them would have been and gone. I wrote to the Tate organiser to complain but was then horrified to find my complaint published in the *Sunday Telegraph* – someone had applied under the Freedom of Information Act to read all correspondence between Turner jurors and the Tate. I didn't dare correspond with anyone after that.

When I finally received the list, I was shocked to find that some of the shows we were supposed to have seen were in places like Basel or Sao Paolo. How were we meant to do that on a total expenses allowance of £250? It was only when we jurors finally met to draw up the shortlist that I discovered that none of the others had actually seen all the eligible shows. One of them told me that you could often see the shows better online. Why didn't I think of that?

The shortlist meeting was held in May, chaired by Nick Serota. Several people had mentioned that I really shouldn't worry my little head because, by some mysterious wizardry, Serota would choose the shortlist himself. However, this wasn't what happened at the meeting; he barely intervened. Each juror was supposed to nominate six artists, which meant that in theory we could have ended up with a shortlist of twenty-four, but all but one of my nominees were brutally rejected by the other jurors. I said of one, Cecily Brown, that she was 'a beautiful colourist' and realised as soon as I said it that I had just shot her fox – beautiful is a despised word in artspeak. But I have the last laugh because Cecily Brown's work *Unmoored from her Reflection* now hangs at the top of the Courtauld's staircase.

Once my nominees had been tossed aside, there was a fairly straightforward consensus and we quickly arrived at a shortlist, which everyone agreed was nicely varied, including as it did a sculptor Rebecca Warren, a painter Tomma Abts, a photographer/filmmaker named Phil Collins and an all-rounder in Mark Titchner. The nominees then had till December to install their Tate shows and we jurors would meet again on prize-giving day to choose the winner.

I'd heard that the final judging could take all day – apparently, when Grayson Perry won in 2003, the jurors were still arguing as guests arrived for the prize-giving dinner. Fortunately, we got it settled in three or four hours and Tomma Abts won. She wasn't my favourite at the nomination stage – though I suspect she was Nick Serota's – but her Tate show, we all agreed, was the best. Then we were dismissed till the evening pre-prize-giving party though we had to promise not to tell anyone or place any bets. Serota told me to come early so I could meet Yoko Ono, who was awarding the prize, and she gave me a brief, gracious audience while dressed as a French mime in a black catsuit and top hat. Then I joined the other jurors and shortlisted artists for a pre-party party which wasn't very exciting because we were all so busy keeping mum. After that we went to the main thrash in the Duveen

Gallery and Yoko Ono presented the prize to Tomma Abts. My year as a juror was over.

I feel quite sad when I remember how thrilled I was to be chosen as a Turner juror – it really didn't prove to be much fun. I saw an awful lot of art – and a lot of it was awful. The benefit of seeing so much art in a comparatively short time however was that I developed a good eye for anything original. So much of what I saw was so derivative that it felt like a real jolt of electricity to come across something genuinely new, so I think it marked an important stage in my little art education.

Would I agree to be a Turner juror again? No.

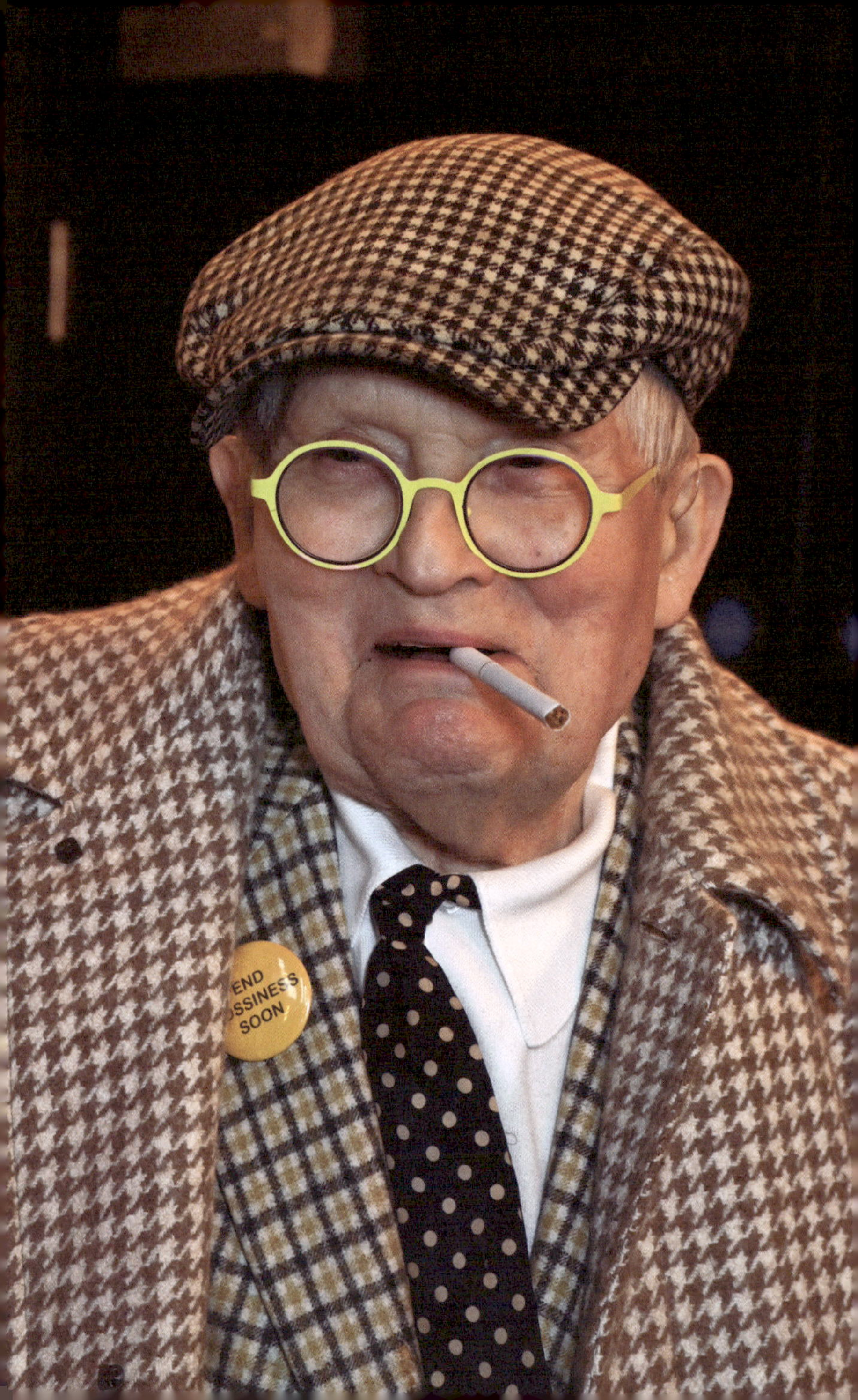
END
OSSINESS
SOON

David Hockney

Am I glad I did it? Yes.

I first interviewed David Hockney back in the sixties for an article in *Queen* entitled '*Where does £10,000 a year get you nowadays?*' £10,000 seemed an amazing sum in those days, and there was much discussion at *Queen* about whether anyone could really earn that much – but Hockney did. He was a very fashionable artist about town, with dyed blond hair, big colourful glasses, and outrageous clothes. He was living in Powys Square, Notting Hill, which was then a very rough neighbourhood, but his house was fabulous, and he was happy showing it off. And this was before he went deaf, so you could have a real conversation.

He moved to Los Angeles soon afterwards, lured by sun and fun and boys, and I went out there to interview him a couple of times in the eighties. He was always very helpful in telling me what airline to fly (Air France) and what hotel to stay at (the Mondrian) so that I could smoke. But his deafness was beginning to encroach on his daily life, to the point that he no longer enjoyed going to parties or listening to music. He told me that he knew he would probably go totally deaf eventually but 'What does it matter? I don't need to listen to paint.'

When I interviewed him again, in 1998, he was still in California, but had just embarked on his great series of Yorkshire paintings. He'd been going to Yorkshire every Christmas to stay with his mother in Bridlington – 'She's ninety-seven so I can't stop now, can I?' – but, in 1996, he learned that one of his oldest friends from Bradford, Jonathan Silver, had been diagnosed with pancreatic cancer. He stayed on through January and February, painting his portrait, and returned in the summer when Jonathan was nearing the end. Every other day he'd drive over the Wolds from his mother's house in Bridlington to Jonathan's house in Wetherby and 'I realised I had fallen in love with the landscape. I was there just as they were beginning to cut the corn, so you'd get these golden fields and then these great big machines, like insects laying eggs, leaving these big bales. Some days were just glorious, the colour was *fantastic*.' He painted against the clock, dawn to dusk, so that he could show the paintings to Jonathan before he died, which he did on 24 September 1997. Returning to Los Angeles, he painted another two Yorkshire landscapes, including *Garrowby Hill*, from memory. These are astonishing works, almost as visionary as Samuel Palmer's, carrying a great freight of emotion – sadness, of course, because Jonathan was dying, but also joy in the beauty of the landscape.

Hockney's mother died in 1999, but he still went back to Bridlington to see his sister, who lived in their mother's house. And then, in 2003, he moved to Bridlington, and took over the house, so that he could paint the changing seasons in Yorkshire. I saw him during this period but in London, at a pro-smoking party held by Forest (Freedom Organisation for the Right to Enjoy Smoking Tobacco) at Boisdale of Belgravia in 2008. He was just coming out for a fag as I was going in – he said they had a roof terrace where you could smoke but it was too crowded and, anyway, he couldn't hear well at parties. I noticed he'd got a wizard new hearing-aid which made it much, much easier to converse. I was telling him about a wonderful Hammershøi exhibition I'd seen, and he told me about other Danish artists, such as Eckersberg, I ought to know about. He told me that he buys all his cigarettes in Baden-Baden, where he goes every few months to take the waters, and smokes Davidoff because they are the longest and Camel

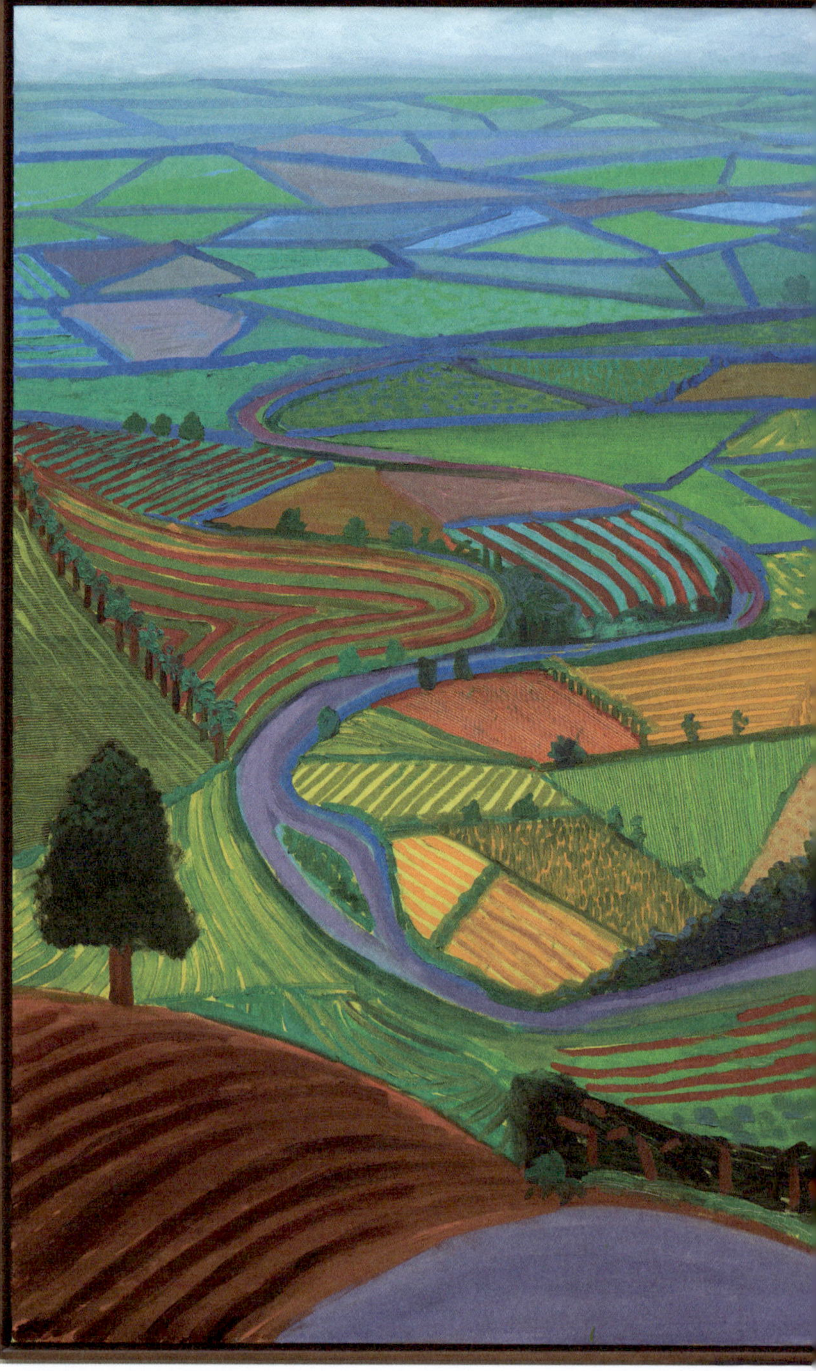

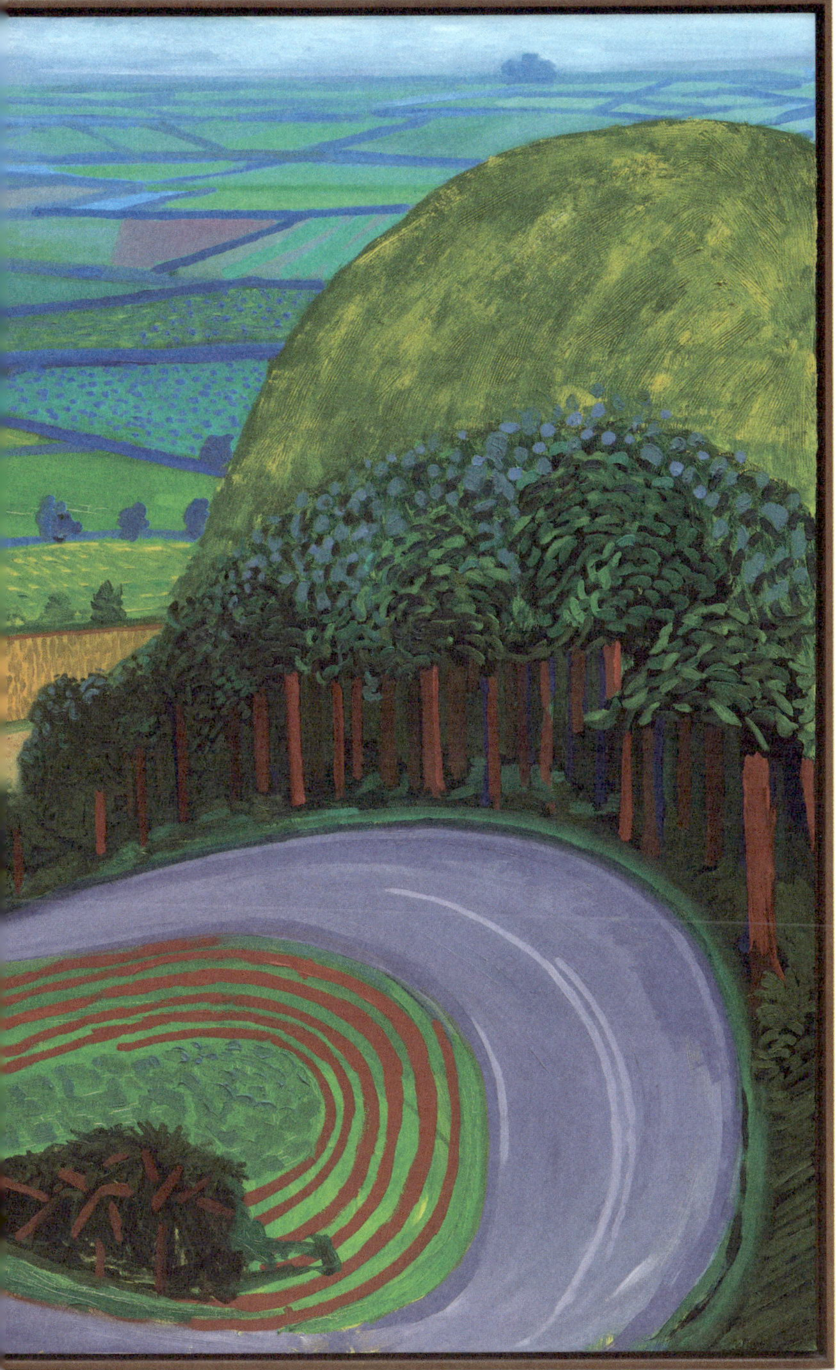

Wide because they are the smoothest, and how he still misses Turkish cigarettes. He was then kidnapped by a gang of people from a nearby art gallery who said he must see their exhibition and he toddled off, still puffing away, and I went in to listen to the Forest speakers . It was then that I got my first sighting of Nigel Farage – I hadn't realised that Forest was associated with UKIP, and wouldn't have gone to the Boisdale party if I'd known.

Alas, I never went to Bridlington, though I admired the great paintings and iPad drawings he made of the changing seasons there. But his Bridlington sojourn ended badly in March 2013 when his young studio assistant Dominic Elliott, son of the local GP, committed suicide by drinking drain cleaner. The inquest found death by misadventure, but the police investigated possible drugs charges. Hockney himself was never implicated – he slept through the incident – but he was obviously upset and returned to Los Angeles, deeply depressed. One day he noticed his studio manager, J-P (Jean-Pierre Gonçalves de Lima), sitting staring at the carpet with his head in his hands, looking exactly as depressed as he felt, and decided to paint his portrait. 'And starting to paint again made me feel better.' So, he decided to paint portraits of all his friends and J-P organised a rota of sitters who would come out for three days, resulting in his great show at the Royal Academy in 2016, *82 Portraits and 1 Still-Life*. The still-life was because one of the friends had to cancel.

I went to Los Angeles to interview him about it, and he was flattered that I'd flown out especially, and even more when I told him I'd had to fly economy but endured it because I was so keen. 'And do you still smoke?' 'Yes of course I do.' We settled down happily in his studio – the size of a tennis court – and puffed away, while he told me about all the great painter-smokers who lived to a ripe old age: Renoir to seventy-eight, Matisse to eighty-four, Monet to eighty-six, Picasso to ninety-one. He showed me his California Medical Marijuana Verification Card that allowed him to buy cannabis for medicinal purposes. He said that obviously he gets more tired as he approaches eighty, but he can still stand at the easel for six hours a day – 'When I'm painting, I feel thirty. It's only when I stop that I know I'm not.'

He wanted to show me an enormous monograph Taschen were publishing called *David Hockney: A Bigger Book* for £1,750 which covered all his work from Bradford to the present day. The early paintings show his astonishingly precocious talent, especially a portrait of his father done when he was seventeen. 'I could draw from the moment I began,' he told me, 'but I learned to draw faster at art school.' Did he think he would be Picasso? 'No! I didn't. I know I'm not. I set out to be a worker and have been a worker.' But he thinks he will be forgotten eventually, as most artists are.

I asked if there was any particular Old Master he turned to for nourishment, and he said 'Rembrandt, Rembrandt's drawings. I'll show you one.' And he fetched a print of a woman teaching a child to walk. 'I think that is the greatest drawing ever made.' I wanted to take a picture but then remembered the sign on his studio wall saying, 'All visitors, please, please. No photography or video. Look with both eyes.' But he very sweetly took my iPhone and photographed it for me.

We had a jolly lunch with J-P and two more of his assistants, and Hockney recited from memory a W. H. Auden poem:

Give me a doctor partridge-plump,
Short in the leg and broad in the rump,
An endomorph with gentle hands
Who'll never make absurd demands
That I abandon all my vices
Nor pull a long face in a crisis,
But with a twinkle in his eye
Will tell me that I have to die.

That was the last time I saw him, but I followed his move to Normandy in 2019 and the latest wonderful iPad drawings and paintings that came out of it. When Covid arrived, my daughter sent me an article about some French research that seemed to show that smokers didn't get Covid. I forwarded it to Hockney in Normandy, and he responded by sending me *reams* of articles about how smokers didn't get Covid, as well as some sweet iPad drawings of his house. He did get Covid eventually – but not badly and he was still able to meet the new King in his Crocs. I love him to bits.

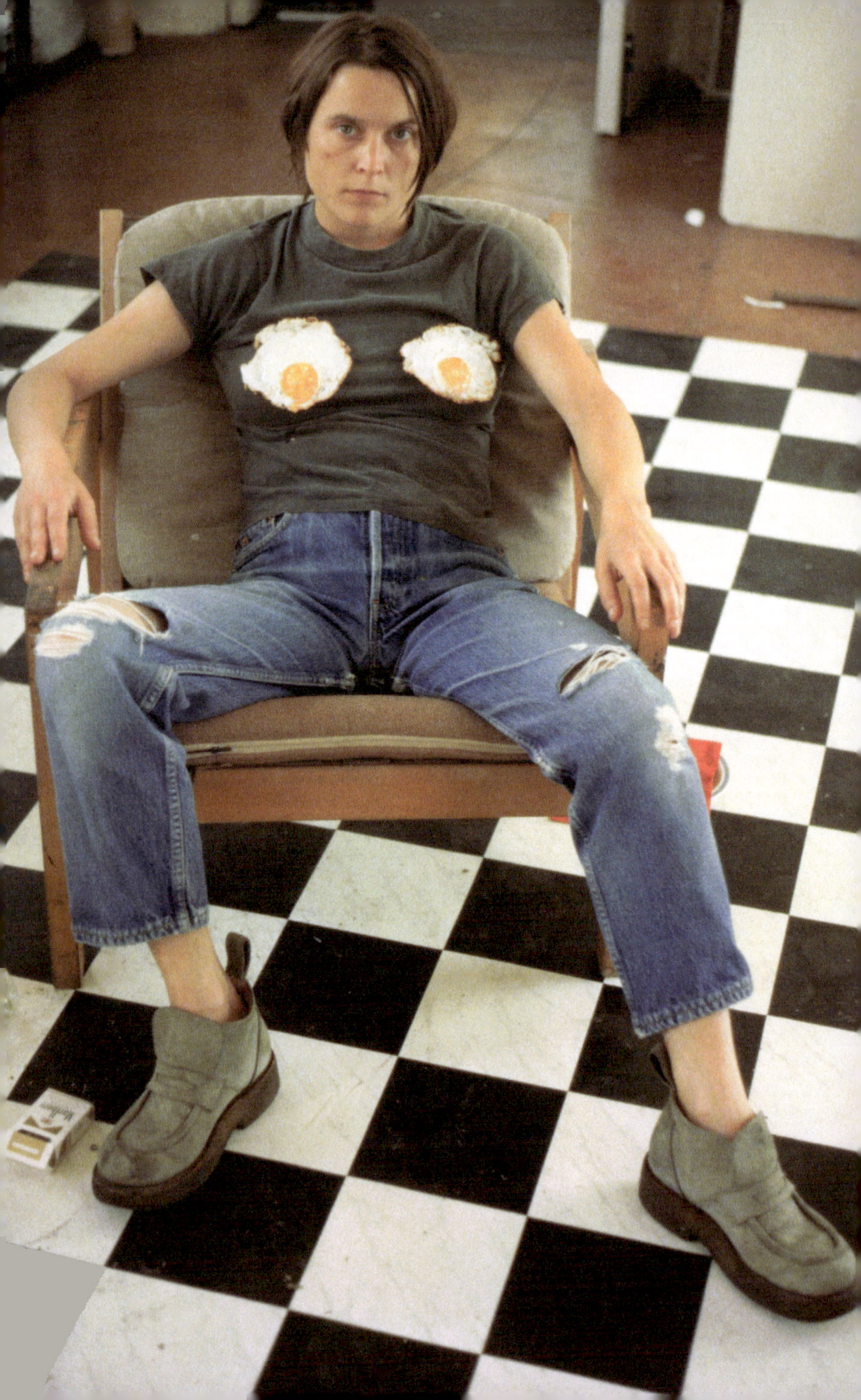

Sarah Lucas

I first met Sarah Lucas in 1999, and quickly decided that not since school had I ever met anyone I so much wanted to call my friend. Sadie Coles, her dealer, invited me to join them at the Cologne Art Fair, where Sadie's gallery stand was devoted entirely to Sarah's work. As it happens, they took very little work with them. Instead they rocked up in Cologne a couple of days before the fair and went shopping. They acquired a sagging gold velour sofa, a plastic table and an office chair from a furniture exchange and then trawled the supermarket for the most obscene-looking sausages, kippers and pumpkins they could find.

I flew out a couple of days later, and Sadie told me to pick up a couple of salami at the airport. 'What sort?' I asked. 'Anything the size of a very big penis.' Then I went to the art fair and was dazzled by its glossiness. We didn't have anything like this in London – this was long before Frieze and the like. Most of the stands had designer furniture and smoothie-chops salesmen in Savile Row suits. But it was Sadie Coles's stand that brought all the strolling crowds of art lovers to a sudden stop. It featured the sofa with two pumpkins placed at breast height, a hideous smoked-meat phallus, and a coat-hanger bearing two fried eggs and what looked like vacuum-packed fish. Sarah told me she'd had terrible trouble getting the fried eggs right – the chef at her hotel couldn't grasp the idea that they had to be overcooked to retain their shape while hanging from a coat hanger, so she'd ended up frying them herself.

There were also the infamous *Beer Can Penises*, mini-sculptures ingeniously fashioned out of two cans stuck together. They sold like hotcakes at DM 999 (about £330); Sadie sold thirty-two of them at the Fair. Between the self-portrait photographs at £6,000, the six pairs of concrete boots at £9,500 each, the *Beer Can Penises* and everything else, I think the gallery must have taken about £50,000 on the first day alone.

In the evening we went to dinner with the Taschens, art publishers whose sitting room featured an enormous Jeff Koons ceramic of a child and two angels pushing a pig. It was my first glimpse of the other side of the art world – not the lonely artists in their studios but the plutocrats who collect their work – and I was glad I had taken Doris Saatchi's advice to concentrate on the artists and not the collectors.

I interviewed Sarah a few months later at her one-bed flat in Highbury, while she was preparing work for her forthcoming Fag Show. She can truthfully be said to have pioneered the use of cigarettes in art: she has covered whole cars in them, and countless garden gnomes, but she has also made some wonderfully elegant self-portraits with the outline of her face drawn in cigarettes. When I saw her, she was sticking Marlboro Lights onto a blown-up yellow life jacket and I was impressed by how meticulously she did it, but also how slowly. I longed to say, 'I could get a sweat shop to do that for you', but she wouldn't approve. 'I know I don't *appear* very perfectionist, and in a lot of ways I'm not, but I want my own brand of not being perfectionist, not someone else's.' She was always annoyed when foreign museums reconstituted her famous *Two Fried Eggs and a Kebab*, and didn't fry the eggs properly or left the salad round the kebab.

Two Fried Eggs and a Kebab, she said, was inspired by reading Andrea Dworkin. She'd been at Goldsmiths with Damien Hirst, but hadn't really flourished there. In fact, she was perhaps the only artist in the Freeze exhibition he organised who wasn't immediately signed up by a gallery. To make matters worse, she was going out with the artist Gary Hume, whose career rocketed while hers flatlined. She made reading Andrea Dworkin then sound a bit like how it must have been for people 'at one time reading Karl Marx.' It unleashed a storm of feminist anger that gave her confidence and a burning desire to address the subject of men's attitude to women. Sadie Coles remembers seeing Sarah's first London show, *Penis Nailed to a Board* – the title taken from a tabloid headline – and found it 'amazing, extraordinary, it felt completely strange and new and a bit dangerous in some way.' Sadie was then working for Anthony d'Offay but when she broke away to set up her own gallery, Sadie Coles HQ, in 1997, Sarah was the first artist she signed. I loved going to Sarah's openings because they were always great parties, often at the St. John restaurant because Fergus and Margot Henderson were her friends.

Years later, Sarah and Sadie would buy a cottage in Suffolk together. It used to be the composer Benjamin Britten's bolthole when life in Aldeburgh got too hectic, and featured a music room. The cottage is deeply hidden among cornfields with no other building in sight and the only sound you can hear is birdsong. I remember a wonderful summer party there that went on all night. Jasper Conran had a very grand house nearby called Flemings Hall that used to belong to the photographer Angus McBean. He rang and invited Sarah to lunch, and obliged when she asked if she could her friends. Fourteen of us, mostly still drunk, descended on Jasper's exquisite manor house, much to the terror of a butler expecting six for something far more civilised.

In 2013, Sarah bought Sadie out of the cottage and moved there pretty much full-time. A year later, it was announced that she would represent Britain at the net year's Venice Biennale. Sadie had been afraid that she wouldn't agree to do it, because she often turned things down (she twice refused to be nominated for the Turner Prize), but needn't have been. She said yes, 'it's a once in a lifetime thing . . . I'll never get asked again.'

In January, I went to Sadie's garage in London to see Sarah making plaster casts of her friends from the waist down for a work called *Muses*. At that stage she'd only made three things for the Biennale. By the time I next saw her in May however she'd already sent all her work off to Venice. She works so quickly.

She said that her Venice show, *I Scream Daddio*, would be all new work, though with some familiar elements such as the use of plaster, body parts, cigarettes and toilets. The big difference was that

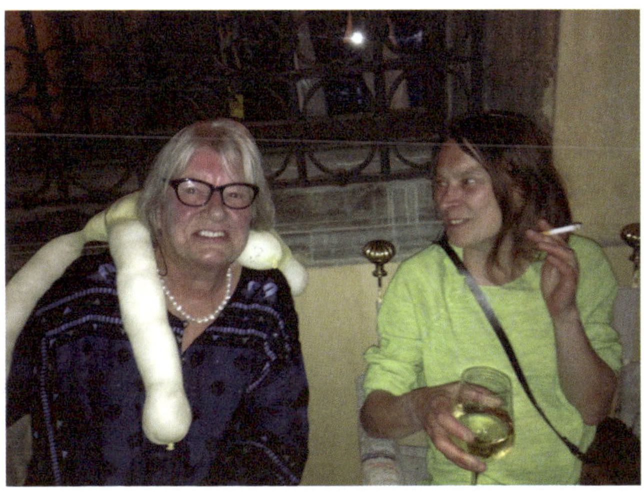

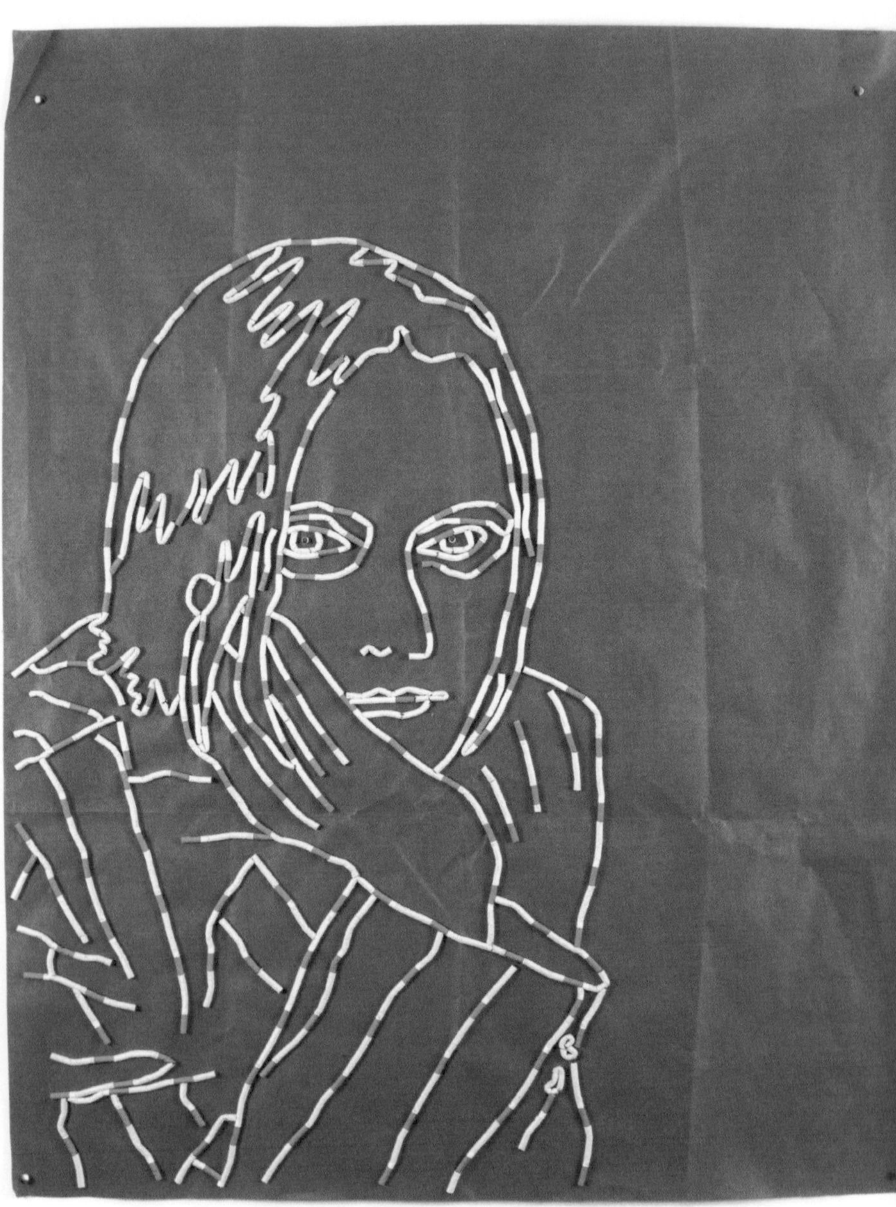

she had brought in more colour, and had painted the whole pavilion yellow – 'I want it to look as if the sun came out.' She sometimes thinks if she'd chosen to do painting instead of sculpture at Goldsmiths she could have been immersed in colour all these years. 'The fact that I became known as this angry sort of tough nut was a fluke really.' In her own words, she never wanted to be angry her whole life – and her Venice show would be 'almost fluffy... a happy show'. It happily received rave reviews. Damien Hirst used to say that Sarah Lucas was the most important of the YBAs, but nowadays he says that she's 'the greatest artist I know'. He owns a big collection of her work, though some of it was destroyed in the Momart fire.

Sarah always said that she never wanted to have a studio because, 'I make art when I feel like it. I like to be cooking or gardening or reading until I stumble across an idea.' So I was surprised when in 2019 she invited me to visit her new studio in Framlingham, a sleepy Suffolk market town.

She explained that some friends had bought the old Conservative Club to turn into an arts centre and she wanted to help so she'd taken the billiards room to use as her studio. 'I just fancied a change. I fancied some company. And it's been good because I've never had that sort of regular, going-to-work feeling, and I like coming into town. I drive in as early as I can, then go home when the light fades and deal with all the emails. It's been good.'

She showed me the stuff she was working on for her new show, *Honey Pie*, then took me to a lovely pub for lunch. It had photographs of Ed Sheeran over the bar – he is the local celebrity. I doubt the regulars know they have another famous artist in their midst. Sarah would certainly never tell them. I couldn't work out why she suddenly looked so much older than when I saw her at the Biennale – but then she took off her cap and showed me. 'It's because of my hair.' It had gone all wispy and streaked with white. Apparently she had alopecia a couple of years back and all her hair fell out. She was terribly upset at first – 'You think, blimey, I'm turning into a *very* old lady overnight.' Now she doesn't feel so bad because it's growing back, but still, 'It's like biting the bullet about getting old.'

She is still ambivalent about her work – 'I never intended it to be my priority. I've never been a massive work-ethic person. I used to think I wouldn't *mind* living off my work but it didn't matter to me that much – and now sometimes it does, sometimes it doesn't. I think in a way I'm on a bit of a pendulum with the art thing – or with anything actually, whether public or private. I definitely like to get right out of it at times.'

The sad thing is that the two artists I most admire – Sarah Lucas and Tracey Emin – are no longer friends. They were the closest possible friends when they launched The Shop in January 1993. Sarah had made some money from selling *Two Fried Eggs and a Kebab* to Charles Saatchi and spent it on the six month lease of a dilapidated house at the top of Brick Lane. She had just split up from Gary Hume and needed somewhere to work, but had decided she didn't in fact want a studio. She wanted a shop. It would be more fun that way: anyone could just drop in. She summoned Tracey (they called themselves 'The Birds' back then) and began selling t-shirts hand-painted with slogans like 'I'm so fucky' and 'Complete arsehole' at £12 each. When one sold, they'd up the price to £15, then £20, and so on. The Shop soon became a much-loved hang-out for artists, famous for its all-night parties. There is a wonderful account of one such party in Gregor Muir's *Lucky Kunst* which is still, by miles, the best art book I know.

Some time after The Shop, Tracey and Sarah fell out, and I've never been able to find out why. The nearest Sarah ever came to explaining was when she told me, 'Tracey was too full on.' I think she disapproved of Tracey's wholehearted embrace of celebrity, the way she would pose for magazines, or fling herself into the gossip columns. Sarah, being rather puritanical, eschewed all that: she thought it debased the whole idea of art. I remember when we went to the Cologne Art Fair, Sarah took me to look at Tracey's drawings which were displayed on another stand, and which she clearly admired.

When Tracey came to my house years later, she was delighted to see her own drawings and monoprints in the hall, but made absolutely no comment when we moved on to the dining room and she saw the big self-portrait photograph of Sarah with a washing line of knickers. She clocked it without comment. Once or twice, in the early years of my friendship with Tracey, I naively hoped to effect a reconciliation but I quickly found that even mentioning Sarah was taboo. When Lucian Freud died, I remember some journalist ringing me, keen to know who I now considered to be our greatest living artist. Without hesitation, I said 'Sarah Lucas' – then quickly found myself wondering whether Tracey would ever speak to me again. Luckily, she did. But it was a dicey moment.

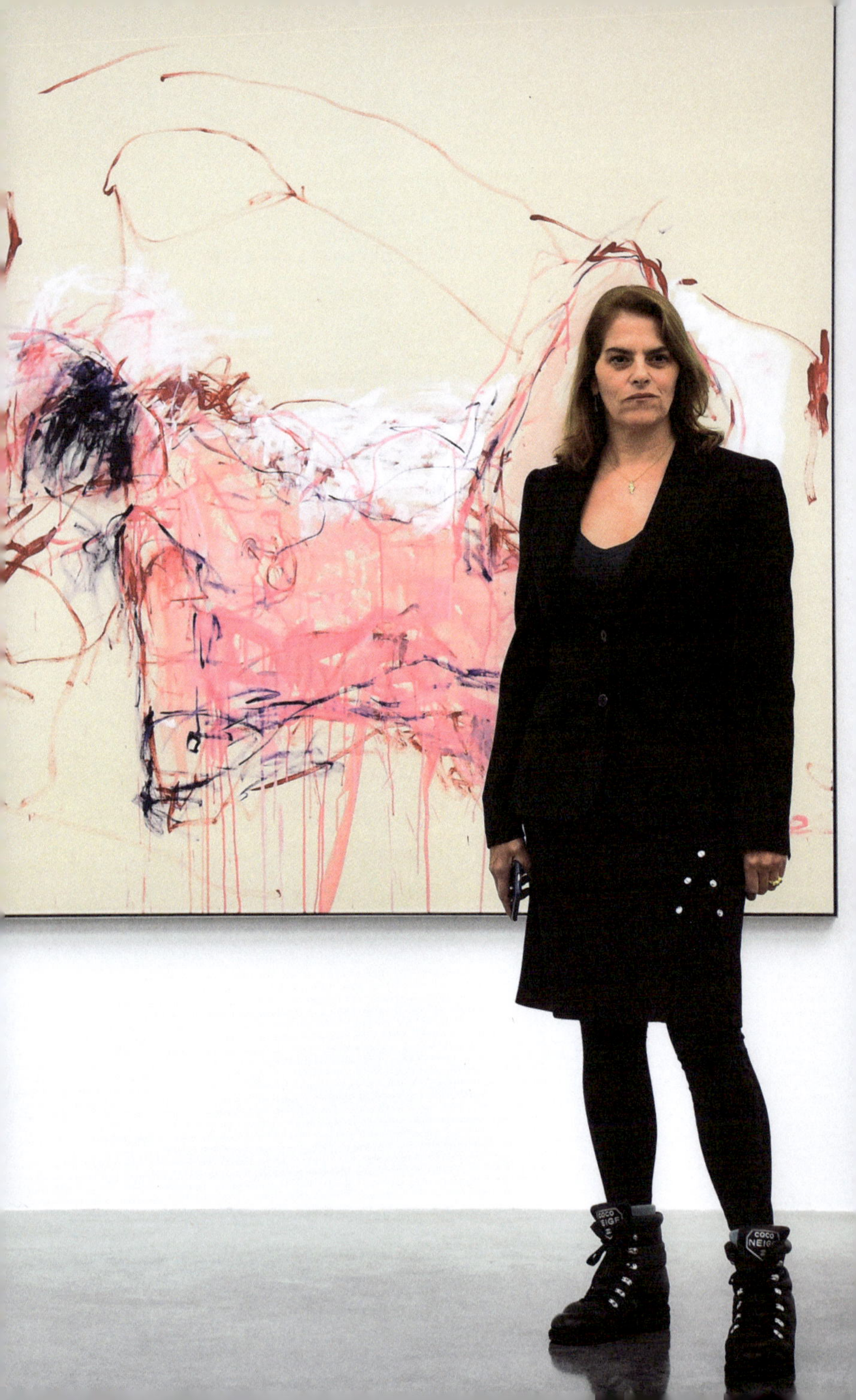

Tracey Emin
The Longest Friendship

Of all the works in the *Sensation* show at the Royal Academy in 1997, the one that really gripped me was Tracey Emin's tent – *Everyone I Have Ever Slept With, 1963–1995*. I thought, improbably, that if I were an artist, that is exactly the artwork I would have liked to make. It took me right back to being a teenager and making a sort of den in my bedroom where I would write down lists of things I found important. It couldn't have been everyone I ever slept with because I'd only slept with two men at that stage, but it could have been books I'd read or places I'd been, or birds I'd seen (I was a secret birdwatcher) – I very much associated being a teenager with making lists in a private place.

So, I already had a great fellow-feeling for Tracey Emin when I went to interview her for the *Observer* in 2001 and we hit it off immediately. We met at her studio off Brick Lane but she quickly dashed me off to her house around the corner. I was, of course, hoping to see her bed – she refused because her boyfriend was still asleep in it. The house was surprisingly neat and tidy except that it had a used condom on the sofa. 'Oh dear,' she said when I pointed it out, 'I knew I should have tidied up.'

Next day she rang and said she had something she wanted to show me, and we should meet at her local, the Golden Heart. I couldn't imagine what she could show me in a pub but it turned out to be her father, Enver Emin. He was waiting to collect his wife, Rose, who'd been sewing blankets in Tracey's studio. He was eighty then but still had a flash of the old ladykiller he must once have been.

I asked him how many children he had. He said five, but Tracey contradicted him and said he'd once told her twenty-three. He also had two wives; he already had a wife and family in London when he met Tracey's mother Pam in Margate and happily commuted between them. He even took both families on holiday to Turkey and installed them in separate hotels. So it was all open and above board?

Yes, he agreed, but Tracey butted in furiously, 'It was never above board, Dad! It's not above board to have two families, right?' I felt she picked this fight every time she saw him. He took it quite calmly.

From then on, Tracey often rang and invited me to lunches and parties. I was still a bit wary of calling her a friend because, apart from anything else, we were a generation apart. But when my husband died in 2003, she kept ringing to check that I was all right and I felt she was a true friend. She was even kinder when my little cat Delilah died in 2012 – as the besotted mother of Docket she totally understood cat grief, whereas my daughters just told me I could always get another cat.

She also proved a good friend at the 2005 Venice Biennale when Gilbert and George were representing Great Britain. George told me they were glad to do it because they'd previously been more honoured abroad than in Britain and he thought the Establishment had 'a problem with us'. Maybe, I suggested, because of all the turds in their work? No, he countered, 'It was because we didn't suck off any members of the Establishment.'

It was a very good show, and followed by a wonderful party at the Pisani Moretta with Rufus Wainwright singing at the piano. Tracey turned up with Ronnie Wood and his wife and I noticed that Ronnie listened attentively to Wainwright's set and congratulated him at the end. Ronnie gave me and Tracey a lift to the Frieze Party, this year in the Palazzo Zenobio. I went in proudly waving my invitation – but Tracey and the Woods were held back by the heavies at the gate. They'd

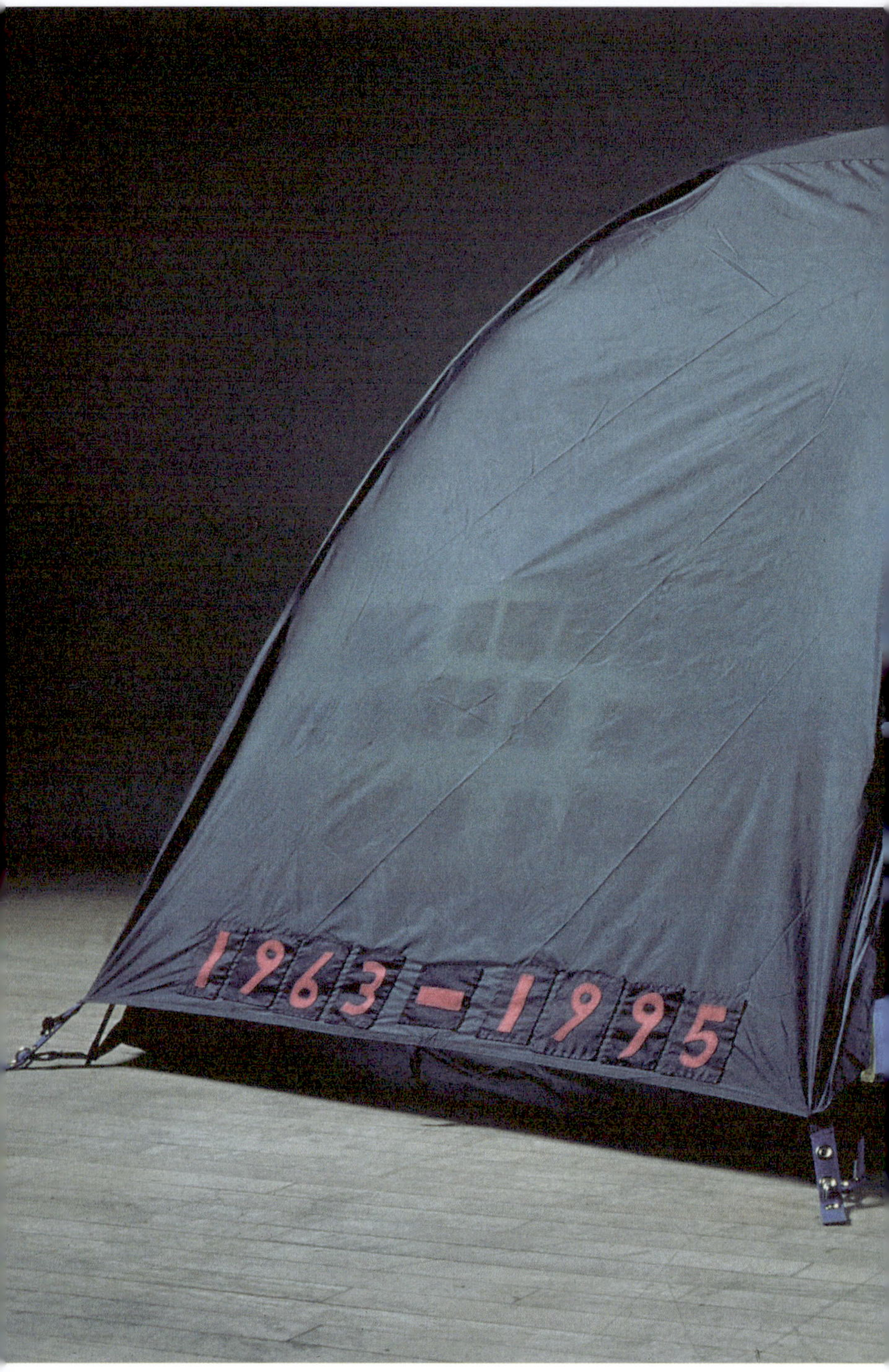
1963 - 1995

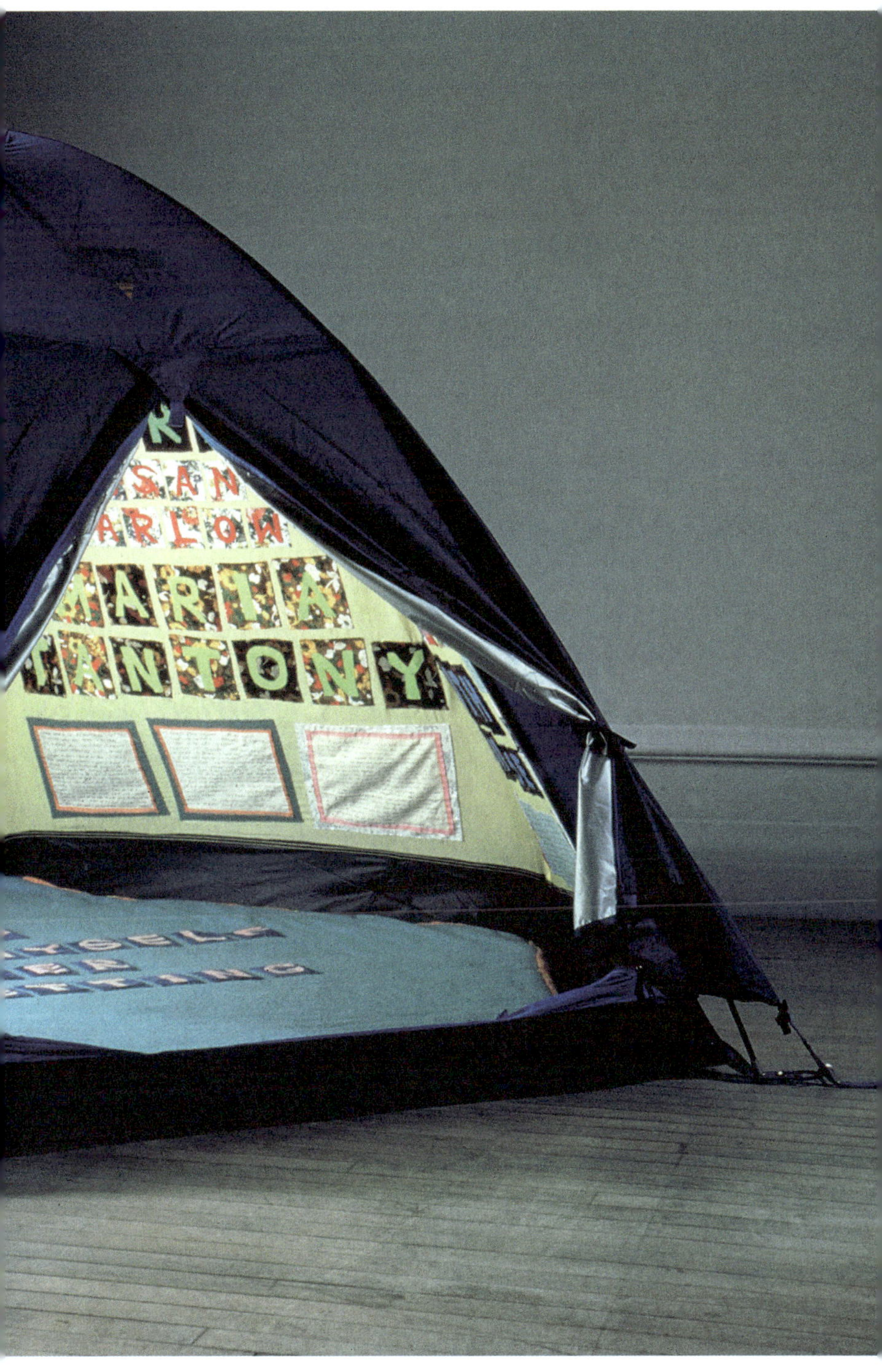
SAN
ARLOW
MARIA
ANTONY
MYSELF
EN
TING

clearly not received their invites, so I was able say, grandly: 'They're with me!' Though it was in fact the Woods's bodyguard who got them in. It was a magical party, in a beautiful garden richly scented with flowers. A rare thing to find in Venice.

While we were in Venice, Tracey said that she'd love to represent Great Britain at the Biennale and I said, 'Oh, yes, wouldn't that be great', never imagining for a moment that it would happen. I thought she was considered too dangerous by the art establishment – too drunk, too loud, too self-publicising. But then she started to clean up her act, writing a weekly column for the *Independent*, and gave a very thoughtful interview on *Desert Island Discs*. She also got to know Andrea Rose, head of visual arts at the British Council, when they were fellow judges on the John Moores Painting Prize in Liverpool, and Rose was impressed by how seriously Tracey took the judging and her brilliant eye for hanging. Still, Tracey thought that the British Council would never choose her – she knew they wanted a woman but she thought it would be Gillian Wearing. But no, in August 2006 the British Council announced that Tracey would be representing Britain at the next Biennale.

She and Andrea Rose went on a recce to Venice and Tracey told her that she wanted the British Pavilion completely renovated, cleaned and painted – which they did, with help from English Heritage. But Tracey also wanted to choose her hotel – and not the sort of discreet long-established hotel the British Council normally chose but maximum luxury on the Lido with her own boat. Andrea Rose told me that it was the first time in her long experience as Biennale Commissioner that she had to go round inspecting five-star hotels and working out the thread count on bedlinen. So, hotel chosen, party date and venue fixed, Tracey spent her autumn and winter quite leisurely, apparently doing no work whatsoever for the Biennale. Instead she concentrated on setting up a new studio-cum-office, and organising her archive. Andrea Rose and her gallerist, Jay Jopling, meanwhile were getting frantic. Tracey told Jopling that she planned to turn the British Pavilion into a swimming pool because there weren't enough swimming pools in Venice and she'd commissioned Richard Rogers to design it and Speedo to sponsor it. She spun the same tale to me for half an hour before cackling, 'Fooled you!'

I still couldn't see any signs of her working for the Biennale. But one day I dropped in to see her on my way to meet friends for lunch in Brick Lane, and she said she'd walk me there, and took me by a circuitous route and suddenly stopped outside a metal door and keyed some numbers into the lock. The shutter rolled up and we were in an echoing hangar full of Tracey paintings – very big, very pale, mostly unfinished. She said she was happy with two of them but not the others, and she was hoping to do a dozen for the Biennale.

She spent the next few months working hard, and I didn't see her again until I met her in Venice a week before the opening in June. She said she'd been very stressed but was now happy, except that British Airways had lost all her luggage and she'd been wearing the same clothes for three days. The pavilion had been completely renovated and looked beautiful and she was happy with the hang – she was just waiting for a few trusted friends; Jay Jopling, Lorcan O'Neill (her gallerist in Italy), old boyfriend Mat Collishaw and Julian Schnabel, her American artist friend – to come and approve it before she signed it off. Then she planned a quick dash home to see Docket, and to collect some more clothes. Seventy friends were coming out for the opening, everyone from Jerry Hall to Sandra Esquilant from the Golden Heart, but Ronnie Wood was on tour with the Rolling Stones and George Michael was playing Wembley. She hadn't invited her family because she wouldn't have time to look after them, so she planned to bring them later, in September. And Scott, her on-off boyfriend, still hadn't shown up.

She said she was going through a midlife crisis and was confused about what she wanted to do with her life. At forty-three, having suffered two botched abortions, she accepted that she would never have children and didn't mind – 'I would rather have my career than children' – and recognised that she was not good at relationships. 'I realised that being an artist is actually quite difficult, and I want to enjoy that difficulty and not feel threatened by it.' She talked about herself non-stop for three hours and then Julian Schnabel arrived and talked about himself non-stop while we made the water-taxi crossing to the Giardini. Even Tracey was silenced by him.

Andrea Rose told me she'd been worried before that Tracey wouldn't produce enough work, but in the end they had plenty to choose from. And she was thrilled by Tracey's restoration of the British Pavilion. 'She has a fantastic spatial sense and is incredibly sensitive to touch and feel.' Which is why, she belatedly realised, they had to go round doing thread counts on hotel bedlinen. 'She's been a dream to work with. What it shows is that she's moved a long way away from the YBAs. She's quite a lady actually!'

Andrea was upset however that Richard Dorment gave Tracey's

show a stinking review in the *Telegraph*, describing it as the worst Biennale offering he'd seen in twenty years. Maybe, I suggested, that was because it was the first time he wasn't on the selection committee. The response of the British press as a whole was mixed, generally cool. It was good then, in a way, that Tracey was so distracted by Scott's messing her around. She didn't read any of the papers until she got home. But I know she didn't enjoy her Biennale.

Many, many years later, when she had moved to Fitzroy Square after her big cancer operation, I found her still obsessing about what she regarded as the failure of her Venice Biennale show. She kept quoting her bad reviews, word for word, and blaming them for her failure to crack the American art market. She tried really very hard – first by taking an apartment in New York and befriending Louise

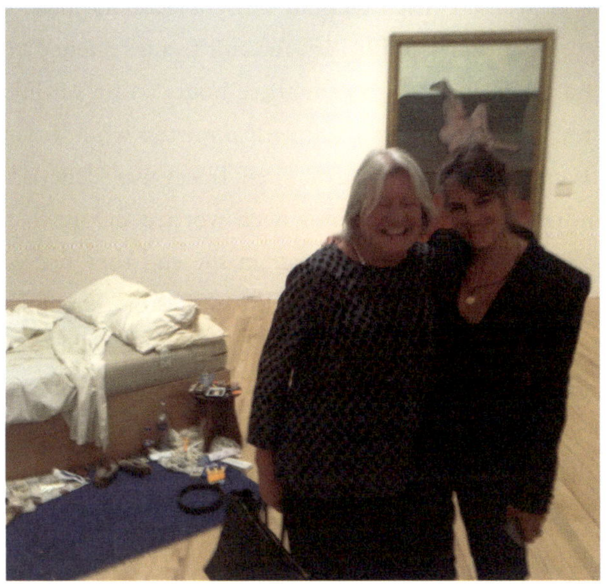

Bourgeois, who gave her some gouaches to embellish, which she very successfully did, before she died. Tracey then turned her attention to Miami, buying a big apartment there on Collins Avenue, mounting a show of her neons to coincide with the Art Fair. It was a very glitzy affair, with red-roped queues and bouncers, and scored another hit with her devotees in the fashion crowd. It did not, however, seriously advance her American career.

When she was a teenager in Margate, a fortune teller told her that she would become very rich – from property. At the time, Tracey didn't even own a room, let alone a flat, so she thought the prediction was crazy, but now, she admits ruefully, she has probably made more money from property than from art. I once asked why she *needed* all these houses and she said it was very simple – when she was a child, her father went bankrupt and his seventy-room Hotel International in Margate, where she'd been treated like a princess, was seized by creditors. Her mother took her and her twin Paul to squat in a staff cottage while she worked as a chambermaid and stole lead from the roof to sell for scrap. Tracey equates property with security and she needs a lot of it.

When I first met her, she had a studio off Brick Lane and the house in Wilkes Street where I found the used condom. Then she moved to Fournier Street, a very exquisite panelled eighteenth-century Spitalfields weaver's house but somehow tight, narrow, on four or five floors, with no big rooms. Parties had to spill out into the courtyard at the back – which was fine for me because she'd created a smoking pavilion – but the house always felt somehow constricted, like a tight vagina.

At the Venice Biennale she told me that she was building a studio in Spitalfields, and that she would have a swimming pool in the basement where I could come and swim. It sounded crazy but she did it: she built a four-floor studio with offices for her staff, a rooftop garden, and a swimming pool in the basement.

She also bought a farmhouse on a hill near Le Lavandou in France and, again, installed a swimming pool. She bought her mother a house in Margate and, when she was trying to conquer the States, she bought an apartment in New York as well as the one in Miami overlooking the beach where turtles laid their eggs.

Then, after she had her operation, she gave up on Spitalfields entirely, sold Fournier Street and her studio, and moved to Fitzroy Square. It was the absolute opposite of the house in Spitalfields – an enormous, bare, stone-floored mausoleum where even the bathroom was bigger than the sitting room in Fournier Street. She said she found the house just after her diagnosis – she'd been to see an osteopath in the square for her bad back and decided that was where she must live. There were no houses on the market but, with typical determination, she got the estate agent to put letters through all the residents' doors asking if they were thinking of moving. Griff Rhys Jones, who owned No. 2, said he was, but not for a year or two, she made him an offer he couldn't refuse and moved there almost immediately after her operation. She still had the builders in when I visited her and I found it all quite sinister. So many bare rooms, empty but for one woman occupant still recovering from cancer and obsessing about what she saw as the failure of her show in Venice.

Just when she'd got the Fitzroy Square house to her liking, she acquired new neighbours who started excavating the building next door to give themselves a four-storey basement, with a garage, a pool, a cinema, etc. The noise of their constant building was unbearable, so Tracey decided to return to Margate to build a house and a studio instead.

I think it suits her, being mad Tracey from Margate again. She has good friends there, too. Carl Freedman has a gallery, her brother Paul, her aunt. She keeps trying to persuade her friends in London to join her – rumour has it that she is buying up most of the town.

In February 2023, Tracey emailed apologies that she hadn't been in touch, but she'd been ill again with septicaemia and various kidney infections. But she was still planning to open her Margate art school in March. I thought this couldn't possibly happen on time, but it did, on 25 March. She bought the old Margate public baths a couple of years ago and converted them into artists' studios, some that she would rent out commercially (TKE Studios) but then ten for TEAR – Tracey Emin Artist Residencies – which her students could use for eighteen months free of charge. She had 800 applicants from all over the world and she got them all to send a video of their work. Then she interviewed the ones who looked promising and asked them about what books they were reading and what was the last exhibition they saw because: 'If people aren't willing to educate themselves, what would be the point of them being here?' It's a wonderful deal for them – not only a free studio and excellent communal kitchen but also free tuition from Tracey and various visiting artists, such as Jake Chapman. Tracey gave them a life-drawing class when they started and told them all to do self-portraits, which they hung on the walls for the opening.

Tracey held a grand opening ceremony, dressed in the red robe and tricorn hat that marks her as a Freewoman of Margate. The 1st Margate Boys' and Girls' Brigade marched down the street, and the town's Social Singing Choir sang Madonna's 'Like a Prayer'. The street was jammed with well-wishers, including Bob Geldof, and TV trucks. I asked if she got lots of local press coverage and she said indignantly, '*world* press, Lynn.' Being a Freewoman of Margate means that she is now entitled to drive a flock of sheep across the beach, and I can't wait to be there when she does it.

People came all day to tour the studios – Antony Gormley was an early visitor. Tracey greeted them from the entrance-hall sofa, where she lay exhausted. She had a stoma-bag tube peeping out under her jacket but told me that she has now finally been given the all-clear from cancer. What an incredible achievement, to set up this art school while still recovering from cancer surgery. It will be great for her because, as she says, being an artist is a lonely life and now she has a whole gang of art students down the road to chat to.

Margate is lucky to have her. As are we all.

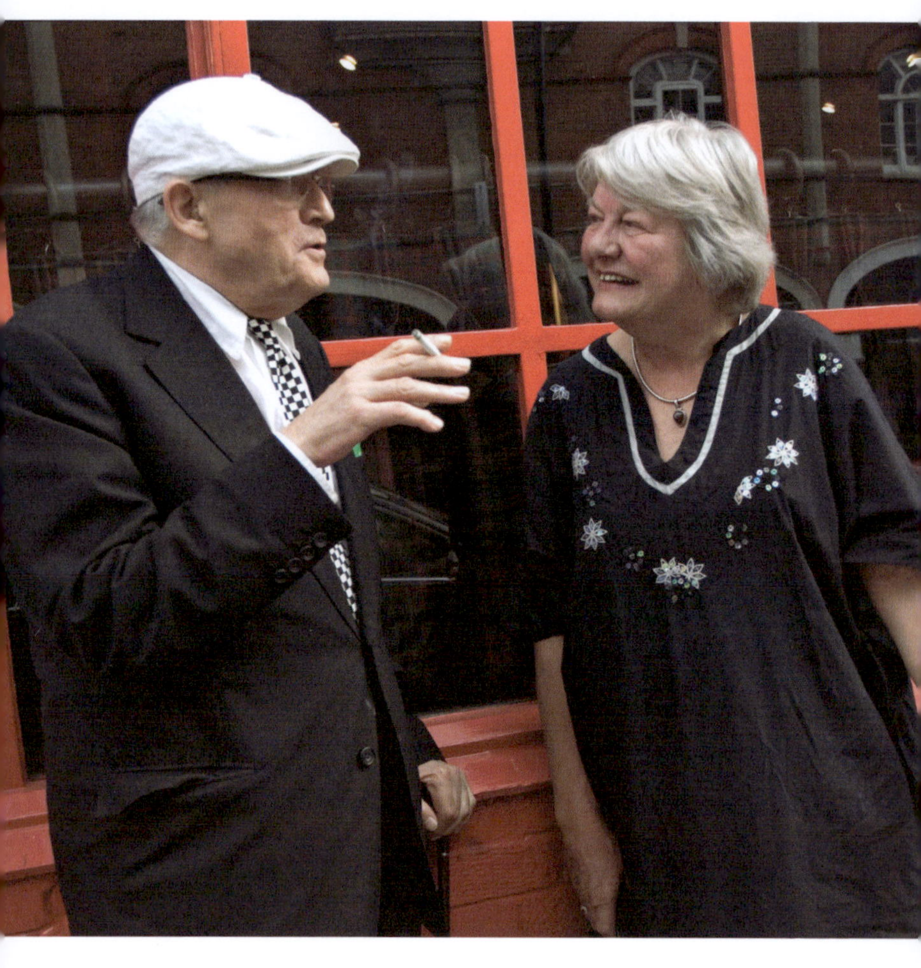

Why Do I Love Artists?

There's a very good novelist called Guy Kennaway (I particularly rec-ommend his *Time to Go*) who often turns up at art parties. He is no more an artist than I am, so I asked why he is such a frequent attender. 'Have you ever been to publishers' parties?' he asked. Yes, of course. 'Well? Writers are so mean and snarky,' he went on, 'they always grumble about their agents or their sales figures, they're bitter and mean-spirited, jealous of other writers. Whereas artists are generous – they want *everyone* to succeed. And also they throw better parties. They're just nicer people altogether, more fun.' I think he's right.

I hugely admire artists for their courage, their willingness to take risks and trust their whole future to their own creativity. I am a rather cautious soul who runs a mile at the idea of burning bridges, so I was awestruck by Michael Landy's *Break Down*, when in 2001 he gathered all his possessions in an empty C&A store on Oxford Street, catalogued all 7,227 items and then got a team of workers to shred them. He made no money from the show and was left only with bags of rubbish. Some of his fellow artists were upset that he shredded artwork they had given him, but he was unrepentant – everything must go.

It was a good, much-needed gesture because by then art was firmly in the grip of mammon. It wasn't until the success of the YBAs in the nineties that anyone thought of art as a money-making career. Very few British artists, apart from Hockney, and then Freud, made a good living from art. Most of them subsisted by living in squats and doing a couple of days' teaching a week (in those far-off days, all schools had art teachers – fancy that!). They regarded it as a bonus if they sold the occasional artwork. But then, with the huge success of the YBAs, the attitude completely changed. Art was suddenly seen as a potentially lucrative career. You could go to art school and be 'the next Tracey Emin' or 'the next Damien Hirst' and galleries rushed to sign up art graduates. This was reflected in the prices at graduate art shows. Back in the sixties, seventies, eighties, you could buy good paintings at graduate shows for £100 or £200 but suddenly the prices jumped tenfold. *Everyone* was a potential Damien Hirst. Except, of course, they weren't. Even if they had some talent, many were at best derivative.

I noticed when I became a Turner Prize jurist that non-artist friends suddenly started consulting me about art. They were always showing me a photograph of some painting they'd seen on sale for £2,000 and asking if I thought it was a good investment. An *investment*, forsooth! These were people who would happily spend £10,000 on a set of curtains, or £100,000 on a kitchen, but a £2,000 painting was only worth buying if it would appreciate in value. How could they be so mean? And why, for God's sake, would you think of art as an investment? You buy pictures because you like them and want to have them on your walls, so you can see them every day. I know there are City syndicates nowadays who often buy artworks and put them straight into storage. I think this is criminal.

So, what has my little art education taught me? Not much, I'm afraid. I've hung out with artists for years now, but I still don't belong in the art room. You have to be an artist; you can't just be a fan. But that's what I admire so much about artists – that they do it. They would rather be an artist, however poor and unknown, than not be one. None of them ever want to retire. Some of them make money, most of them don't, but art is what keeps them going. When you meet, say, bankers or dentists (dentists above all) they always tell you their plans for what they'll do when they retire, some hobby they'll pursue. I've never met an artist who had a hobby, apart from Frank Stella who told me he only carried on painting to feed his horse-racing habit, but even he was pretty old by then. Most artists just want to keep making art. Marc Quinn told me that he had to make it a rule to leave his studio at six, otherwise he would go on painting all night. Tracey *does* paint all night when she is on a roll. Hockney, in his eighties, still dashes outside if there is a particularly good moon to paint. Art definitely keeps you young and engaged.

So that is why I envy artists: they have this consuming passion that will last them all their lives.

List of Illustrations

(in order of appearance)

Portrait of Lynn Barber. Photograph by © Harry Borden, 2016. Courtesy of Harry Borden.

Portrait of Phyllida Barlow. c. 2012. Photograph by © Eamonn McCabe/Popperfoto, via Getty Images.

untitled: dock: 5stockadecrates, 2014. Installation view. Duveen Commission, Tate Britain, London, UK, 2014 © Phyllida Barlow. Photograph by © Alex Delfanne. Courtesy of the artist and Hauser & Wirth.

Portrait of Salvador Dali. Photograph by © Roger Higgins, 1965, via Alamy.

Christo explains how he will wrap several Florida islands. Photograph by Jacques M. Chenet/CORBIS, 1980-83, via Getty Images.

Surrounded Islands, Biscayne Bay, Greater Miami, Florida, 1980-83. Christo and Jeanne-Claude, 1983. Photograph by Wolfgang Volz/LAIF/Camera Press. Courtesy of Christo and Jeanne-Claude.

Running Fence, California, Sonoma and Marin Counties, 1972-76. Christo and Jeanne-Claude, 1976. Photograph by Wolfgang Volz/LAIF/Camera Press. Courtesy of Christo and Jeanne-Claude.

Light Headed, 1991. Gilbert & George, Tate. Artists Rooms acquired jointly with the National Galleries of Scotland through The d'Offay Donation, with assistance from the National Heritage Memorial Fund and the Art Fund, 2008. Courtesy © Gilbert & George and Tate.

L-R: Ian Davenport, Damien Hirst, Angela Bulloch, Fiona Rae, Stephen Park, Anya Gallaccio, Sarah Lucas and Gary Hume prior to Freeze private view, August 1988. Photograph by © Abigail Lane. Courtesy of DACS/Artimage.

Jake and Dinos Chapman attend a photo call for their exhibition Come And See at the Serpentine Sackler Gallery, 2013. Photograph by Rune Hellestad/Corbis, via Getty Images.

Mummy & Daddy Chapman, 2009. © Jake and Dinos Chapman. Courtesy of the artists.

Zygotic acceleration, Biogenetic de-sublimated libidinal model (enlarged x1000), 1995. © Jake and Dinos Chapman. Courtesy of the artists.

Jake and Dinos Chapman's Tragic Anatomies are seen at The Thinking Big auction exhibition at the Sorting Office on October 11, 2013 in London, England. Photograph by © Peter Macdiarmid, via Getty Images.

Rachel Whiteread with House, 1993. Photograph by In Pictures Ltd./Corbis, via Getty Images.

Rachel Whiteread's House, 1993. Photograph by © Richard Baker/In Pictures, via Getty Images.

Working at Night (Lucian Freud), 2005. Photograph by © David Dawson/Private Collection. All rights reserved 2024, via Bridgeman Images.

Gillian Ayres in her studio. Photograph by © Antonio Olmos. Courtesy of Antonio Olmos.

Photograph of Lynn Barber's paintings by Gillian Ayres. Photograph by © Noel Faucett/Editioned. Courtesy of Lynn Barber and Noel Faucett, 2023.

Howard Hodgkin poses next to a detail of his painting 'Where The Deer And The Antelope Play 2001-2007' at Modern Art Oxford, June 17, 2010 in Oxford, England. Photograph by © Christopher Furlong, via Getty Images.

Portrait of Grayson Perry. Photograph by © Kathy De Witt. All rights reserved 2024, via Bridgeman Images.

Hold Your Beliefs Lightly, 2011. © Grayson Perry. Courtesy of the artist.

Recipe for Humanity, 2005. © Grayson Perry. Courtesy of the artist.

Maggi Hambling at the Cheltenham Literary Festival, 2015. Photograph by © WENN Rights Ltd, via Alamy.

'A Conversation with Oscar Wilde' by Maggi Hambling, Adelaide Street, London. Photograph by © View Pictures/© Maggi Hambling. All rights reserved 2024, via Bridgeman Images.

Henrietta 7/6/98 (IV), 1998. © Maggi Hambling. Courtesy of British Museum, London.

Placards designed by Charles Thomson, quoting Lynn Barber; Demonstration against the Turner Prize outside Tate Britain, 4 December 2006. Left: Eamon Everall, artist, one of 13 founder members of the original Stuckists group Right: Frederico Penteado, artist, founder of the Kennington Stuckist group. Photograph by © Charles Thomson, 2005. Courtesy of Charles Thomson.

David Hockney attends the Gala Opening of "David Hockney: Bigger & Closer (not smaller & further away)" at Lightroom, February 21, 2023 in London, England. Photograph by © Dave Benett, via Getty Images.

Garrowby Hill, 1998. © David Hockney. Photograph by Prudence Cuming Associates/Museum of Fine Arts, Boston.

Lynn Barber and David Hockney. Photograph by © Sophia Evans/the *Guardian*, via Eyevine.

Self-Portrait with Fried Eggs, 1996. © Sarah Lucas. Courtesy of Sadie Coles HQ, London.

Lynn Barber with Sarah Lucas. Courtesy of Lynn Barber.

Self-Portrait With Cigarettes, 2000. © Sarah Lucas. Courtesy of Sadie Coles HQ, London

Tracey Emin with It was all too Much during a preview of her A Fortnight of Tears, at the White Cube in Bermondsey, London. Photograph by © PA Images, via Alamy.

Everyone I Have Ever Slept With 1963-1995. © Tracey Emin. All Rights reserved, DACS/Artimage, 2023. Courtesy of White Cube, London.

Lynn Barber with Tracey Emin. Courtesy of Lynn Barber.